# CONTENTS

Photos in this book by Alan and Joann Riley except those by Vince Serbin, pages 7, 11.

## KW-013 ISBN 0-87666-675-6

© 1979 by T.F.H. Publications, Inc.

Distributed in the U.S. by T.F.H. Publications, Inc., 211 West Sylvania Avenue, P.O. Box 427, Neptune, N.J. 07753; in England by T.F.H. (Gt. Britain) Ltd., 13 Nutley Lane, Reigate, Surrey; in Canada to the book store and library trade by Beaverbooks, 953 Dillingham Road, Pickering, Ontario L1W 1Z7; in Canada to the pet trade by Rolf C. Hagen Ltd., 3225 Sartelon Street, Montreal 382, Quebec; in Southeast Asia by Y.W. Ong, 9 Lorong 36 Geylang, Singapore 14; in Australia and the South Pacific by Pet Imports Pty. Ltd., P.O. Box 149, Brookvale 2100, N.S.W., Australia; in South Africa by Valiant Publishers (Pty.) Ltd., P.O. Box 78236, Sandton City, 2146, South Africa; Published by T.F.H. Publications, Inc., Ltd., The British Crown Colony of Hong Kong.

# TAKING YOUR DOG
# BACKPACKING

by ALAN and JOANN RILEY

The Newfoundland, one of the northern breeds of working dogs, bred for heavy work in harsh climates, is well-suited for backpacking over a number of different terrains.

The Malamute, descended from a heritage of use as a beast of burden, is both physically and temperamentally suited for backpacking and hiking.

7

# Acknowledgements

We wish to thank Kitty Drury for her continued interest in this activity and her early encouragement to share it with others.

# Dedication

This manual is gratefully dedicated to two Newfoundland dogs: to "Golly"—teacher, companion and steadfast partner, who opened gates to the wilderness and to the heart; and to his daughter "Katrynka"—generous and intrepid leader whose single-minded resolve once stood alone to roll back fate's darkest shade.

# Introduction

Early explorers who came to the upper reaches of the North American continent found the Indians and Eskimos using dogs to haul sleds. An experienced team could pull a load that equals twice its weight. A loaded team could average three miles per hour and work an eight hour haul, day after day indefinitely. The average distance traveled, from full load at the beginning of the trip to nearly empty at the end, was 20 miles per day.

Since these dogs also assisted hunters in locating seals, provided companionship and protection and could be eaten in an emergency, they were an indispensable tool for travel and survival. In summer when the ice and snow had disappeared the dogs were loaded with makeshift packs. Normally they were loaded to about one-third of their own weight, but there are accounts of dogs being burdened up to their own weight on short hauls and portages.

The animals used in this fashion were short-coupled, heavily boned and wide of rib. Their heavy double coats gave their skin protection from the straps and corners of a load. Their broad furry paws gave good traction relative to their size and weight. Year-round use accustomed their paws, muscles and cardiovascular systems to hard work.

Their role was primarily one of being a beast of burden. Care was casual and minimal. Injured dogs were killed and often fed to their mates. Little seemed to be made of their peripheral usefulness. With the exception of the lead dog, or lead team of two dogs, the bonding between man and dog was weak.

During the invasion of the North by gold seekers, speculators and their hangers-on, most newcomers adopted the same attitude toward these animals. But perceptive individuals, noticing the many contributions sled-pack dogs made to man's welfare in that harsh environment, studied their work and attributes and began the sport of "dog mushing." Breeding programs and team competitions were underway at the turn of the century.

The emphasis in literature is all on sledding since it was fast and

9

(1) Originally used for hauling and other heavy jobs over icy, harsh ground, the Newfoundland has wide paws, and paw pads that toughen with hiking over rugged rock slides. (2) Their heavy coats protect these Newfoundlands from severe weather, providing insulation even in extreme cold. (3) Once considered mainly a beast of burden, the emotional bonding between this breed and man was largely ignored until the turn of the century when further-reaching aspects of the Malamute's temperament began to be developed.

1
2

3

relatively economical with respect to loads. However, we do know that from the earliest times to the present, men used dogs regularly to transport goods by pack. What we learn about packing comes mostly in fragments from the accounts and letters of early settlers who mention their dogs when they describe how they moved skins, flour and hardware into and out of camp. More recent descriptions of dogs as pack animals refer to military use. Photographs show German Shepherd Dogs and some of the Belgian breeds on the front lines of World War I, often equipped with packs carrying the medical corps insignia. St. Bernards, Great Pyrenees and Newfoundlands were given special training during World War II for pack use in Alaska and the Aleutians.

The growing network of air freight, big-engined motor boats and roadways casts a long shadow over the future of the dog for individually-packed hauling. Even if the energy shortage and the problem of mechanical breakdowns have rebuilt interest in the use of dog teams for winter sledding, the shortening of distance and disturbances of traditional life styles relegate both sledding and dog packing to only the rare few.

In the last ten years the interest in backpacking with a dog as a member of a hiking party has grown rapidly. The reasons are clear. Dogs are pleasant company. They enjoy the action and environment of a hike and they provide a measure of protection on the trail and in the camp. As more people discover the satisfactions of cross-country hiking and snowshoeing they seek to introduce their pets to these activities.

Nearly every sporting goods merchant catering to hiking, climbing and canoeing interests displays a dog pack. It is stuffed neatly with papers and fits snugly over the rolled ground pad that substitutes for a dog. The appeal must be successful for any day hike on a popular route contains parties with dogs. Some dogs lurk uncomfortably, dragging behind under a shifting load. Others scatter out far ahead rooting or baying out at any wildlife they uncover. In 14 years, and many miles on and off trails in the Northeast, we have encountered only one packer who had his dogs under control, well-packed and fully at ease with their task.

In the far North, dog packing was common but in southern Canada and the lower forty-eight states there is no experience to guide newcomers. As a result, the party that includes a dog is usually a nuisance to itself, other parties and wildlife. Dogs once welcome everywhere in the wilderness are now regulated out of all trail areas in national parks and are restricted to a selected few vehicle camp sites under strict control. It may only be a matter of time before national forests take the same action beginning with major hiker routes and extending finally to closure at forest boundaries. This sequence of events could be stopped if rangers and forest managers were confident that people who arrive with dogs would keep them under control.

A growing population multiplied by the growing number of people especially interested in outdoor experience must now be scheduled into and out of wilderness areas. In some cases they must designate each night's camping location. In all cases, parties will meet other parties and share the limited areas appropriate for travel and camping. The frontier is gone, and with it goes much of the freedom, privacy and careless use of natural resources vast wilderness once offered to its rare travelers.

Those of us who now carry on with packing in the lower forty-eight states are not freight packers. It is the combination of assets, once overlooked or taken for granted in working dogs that interests us most—loyalty, mutual communication and companionship. We are a departure. Our livelihood does not depend on our dogs, but there are situations where our lives still do. At those moments and during the long and pleasant spaces between, we share with our dogs a full measure of the best traditions between two distinct species in Earth's family.

The time has come, for those of us who have experienced packing with dogs, to share our information with those who are beginning. You and your dogs will become skillful far sooner than we who launched into it on a trial and error basis. You will also be warned of a few special hazards and be able to avoid them. The activity is both simple and pleasurable. While this is all it appears to be on the surface, as you move into it you will make discoveries about communication and bonding between humans and dogs that will add more to the experience than words can tell.

2

(1) For a packing dog to be an enjoyable companion, he must be under control at all times. Here, one of the author's dogs responds to a hand signal. (2) Mutual trust and sensitivity to needs of both dog and human are even more important when backpacking with dogs; for a human's life may literally depend upon the well-honed instincts of his pet. (3) The usual place for packing dogs is behind their master who assumes the role of leader.

3

This breed of working dog, used by some to haul freight, is included in the authors' hikes, primarily for the companionship and added dimension to the human senses of sight and sound they provide.

A typical command-obey relationship can flourish, on the trail, to one that becomes an understanding between equals and which works to a mutual advantage for both dog and master.

# I The Concept

The authors have a particular point of view on dog packing. We recognize there are others that may be more appropriate for other dog owners or the requirements of specialized packing tasks. We do not use our dogs primarily as freight haulers. For us, companionship is the fundamental reason for having them along. We see the advantages of protection and extra sensitivity to sound and smell as valuable additions. Hauling comes a distant last since we are used to carrying what we need ourselves.

Hauling freight, as some northern dogs are required to do in the summer as well as winter, involves a variation of the travois pole skids or bulky packs wound above and around the dog's chest with line or straps. (A travois is a primitive vehicle that was used by Indian tribes from North America; it was actually two poles that supported a frame and was dragged across the ground by an Indian or one of his animals). Under a pack, 70 pound dogs are commonly loaded with 50 or 60 pounds of gear and move a full work day for many days or even weeks across the tundra and boreal forests of the Far North. Even in winter, dogs are occasionally packed instead of being harnessed to a sled. Their build, in combination with their inbred sturdiness and endurance, allows them to perform extraordinary tasks routinely.

An owner of any medium or large sized dog in good health could probably condition his animal to this high standard. However, in the terrain of the continental states, canoes, horses, mules and burros can do a much better job of moving freight. Since these animals are readily available, the use of a dog as a freight hauler is an exercise in nostalgia.

The reasons for not loading a dog heavily are clear. By burdening him with a load set to meet his limits of strength, you take away the balance and agility needed for a rock scramble or penetrating the occasional maze of downed timber. A huge pack will not fit small openings. You spend a good deal of time finding a route your dogs can manage, or unpacking and repacking a stripped load. Crossing fast water with a heavy pack is usually impossible unless the stream bed is very shallow. The speed and maneuverability your dog needs in an emergency is gone. So too is much of the joy and spontaneity that makes him a pleasant companion.

We go to the wilderness for pleasure. Our intention is to share that pleasure with our dogs. We seek to minimize the extra effort required to live and travel safely in an environment supremely indifferent to human needs. We carry only what we need and so do our dogs. On a typical day hike our dogs will carry only four or five pounds. On a larger hike that load will increase to include food and pans. On rare occasions, it is necessary to carry water for a day or two. That condition substantially adds to their burden and they may carry as much as 25 or 30 pounds. Our current Newfoundlands weigh from 110 to 145 pounds. It would be easy to put more weight on them, but our choice is to protect all of the competence, mobility and enthusiasm they normally have. With careful planning they can go for a whole week carrying no more than 25 pounds, including a day or two when a dry camp is necessary.

Our concept is to form a working partnership. What begins as a master-servant command-and-obey relationship evolves into a partnership of equals. Experience taught us that our dogs have capacities to know, and to communicate what they know, far surpassing our expectations. We realize now that for the first few years of packing work, we effectively masked important contributions the dogs could make by insisting on the typical command-obey relationship. They knew more than we gave them credit for. They learned it more quickly than we expected and they could extend our knowledge of the environment if we backed off and allowed them to inform us.

A veteran trail dog does not need instructions. Once the pack is on his back, he and you are on a plane where speech is not necessary unless an unusual circumstance arises. We talk to the dogs because we are alone with them. They talk back, as dogs do, to express pleasure, excitement or affection. With experienced dogs the communication necessary for trail work is expressed through stance and we watch a veteran dog closely. More accurately, we listen intently, for when we move, he is behind. If we cannot hear him close behind, we turn to see why he has stopped. If he has a smell that interests him, we wait until he is satisfied with his investigation. If he is erect, mouth closed to listen, we too remain silent and unmoving until he is satisfied. Normally, we smell and hear nothing. But if this pattern persists, we know we are in the immediate vicinity of a creature or a condition that might be worth paying attention to. In the past, when we failed to heed these signals, we missed opportunities for animal and bird sightings. We now honor them.

Each new pup moves gradually from a consistent teach-and-learn routine toward increasing independence. The basics are quickly entrenched: do not attack living creatures, do not rush the available water, no frolicking until the pack is off, watch the hiker, stay close behind but keep off the tail of snowshoes and the backs of shoes. These rules are simple matters of citizenship, but they have to be observed under the difficult circumstances of bad footing, swift currents and the immediate presence of pack horses, other hikers with dogs and wild creatures. We make no claims of perfect observance. The sight of an approaching dog sled team with its frantic yips brings our dogs forward, alert. They are more

Usually one dog, or even two, in a hiking party is sufficient, this being an easy number to control. But as the hiker's experience with dogs increases, and the veteran trail dog takes over an instinctive training of the newcomer by virtue of his example, a hiking party may feel comfortable with more. However, it is not recommended that more than three be used as they crowd a trail when passing other parties, and are difficult to keep track of in rough water crossings.

familiar with the challenge of many voices than they are with the sight of a team underway. We take a firm hold on the collar and hope the lead dog knows his job as well as our dogs know theirs. We also hold the dogs in the presence of a pack string on a narrow trail. To put a human or animal life in jeopardy to satisfy pride is a foolish gamble. Horses have the inside. The outside leaves no room for whims and errors. All in all, we can say that we travel in confidence knowing that most unusual situations will not upset long established habits.

Full partnership arrives when you realize that what the dog can do for you he does routinely: calling your attention to trails, scat (animal droppings) and animals you would have missed; hanging back and watching intently as you negotiate an exposed or difficult stretch; taking care to keep his distance; standing firm under the onslaught of a sudden thunderstorm; barking an alert to signal the presence of a bear approaching camp; always moving alongside to be first to meet a perceived threat on the trail; meeting that perceived threat with no belligerence as strangers and their animals make acknowledged contact.

As his experience grows, you are aware that you have given no commands but the dog is consistently where you need him to be, doing the things you need him to do. Finally, you recognize how often you watch him for his signals to you. The mutual dependency and the partnership are complete. Getting the dog and yourself to that point is what the rest of this book is about.

The hiking party stops to make an adjustment on the dog's pack. The dogs should be checked periodically to make sure burrs are not adhering in tight places, and that the neck straps are not binding them.

In a moment of play along the trail, a dog brings a "prize," a piece of hiker's clothing, to his master.

# II Pack and Gear

The first requirement is to be equipped with clothing and tools that best serve the needs of safety and reasonable comfort. See Appendix.

There are many ready-made dog packs now available. A pattern and instructions for making your own pack are included in Appendix . Materials are available in any outdoor shop in major cities.

The important thing is to get a pack that: 1) fits the dog, 2) does not impede his movement, 3) stays in place, 4) is durable and 5) comes on and off easily. The last is especially important where it is cold. The job should be done without having to remove the gloves worn inside an outer mitt. If you make your own pack, you will have a better chance of meeting these requirements.

The first thing the hiker will discover when using a dog pack is

It is a good idea to equip packs with drain grommets at the bottom of the pockets. When your hike calls for entering water, it will not be necessary to stop each time to empty water out of the pockets. The contents inside have all been routinely wrapped to be watertight, so they will pose no problem.

the importance of loading it evenly. One side should be balanced by the weight on the opposite side. This is easily accomplished by adding a few rounded stones to the pocket on the lighter side—rounded so as not to dig into the dog's ribs as he moves.

The first things to go into the dog's packs are equivalent to what the hiker needs for his own needs. A water and food pan, a long lead (about 12 feet), pliers with a cutting edge below the teeth (for porcupine quills) and any extra food, water or first aid supplies appropriate for a longer trip. A Cutter kit or an antivenin kit might be needed in rattlesnake country. The hiker should educate himself on this topic before he makes a choice of treatments. Vinegar is useful if camp is to be made where skunks or porcupines are commonly found. Dogs can carry water easily in military-type fabric two quart containers. These are pliable and do not dig into the dogs' ribs. They collapse into a small space when not in use, and are very durable. The caps will not leak despite being knocked about.

A hobble or restraint is needed in case the dog is incapacitated and must be carried out. While one could be fashioned on the spot using line, it would not be suitable for a long, uncomfortable carry.

It is also useful to add a few "D" rings to the outside of the pack for lashing awkward objects. They may not be used often, but on occasion it is very handy to have the dogs carry snowshoes, a ground mat or camp shovel. If dogs are expected to enter water regularly, two drain-hole grommets should be put into the bottom of each pocket. That will make it unnecessary to unload and empty the water before continuing on. Materials to be kept dry have to be packed watertight, anyway.

A six-foot hiking pole has many uses. One of them is as a training aid, to bar the novice dog's natural tendency to charge out in front. Its use will be discussed in more detail later. Booties may be useful in certain conditions of crusted snow, broken ice or wet snow; however they hamper traction in most situations and are hard for dogs to get used to. If those conditions were to arise without warning, extra wool socks and heavy fabric tape could serve the same purpose temporarily.

See Appendix for a detailed list of equipment.

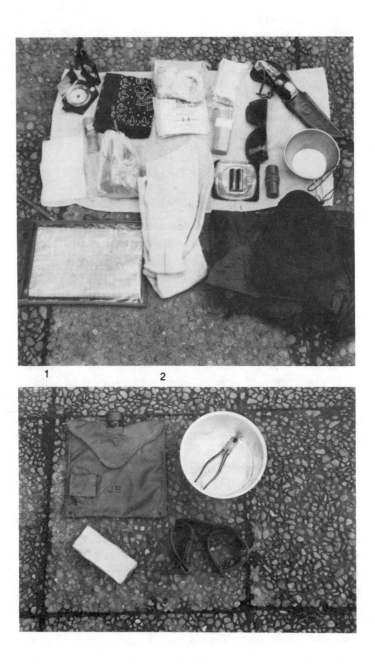

1 2

(1) Contents of a pack showing (from top l. to r.) a sighting compass; bandana; first aid kit; emergency blanket; camp knife; (next row) insect stick; emergency food pack; wool socks; flashlight; sunglasses, drinking cup; (below right) watertight match case; wool cap; jacket with hood. (2) Dog pack containing: (top left) collapsible canteen with halazone tablets in pocket; food pan and pliers; (bottom left) antivenin kit; hobble. The hobble is used only if the animal must be carried on the hiker's shoulders. (3) Day pack of light weight fabric used for shorter distances. (4) Freight pack of heavier fabric with larger pockets and more "D" rings, used for long hauls. (5) Dog's day and freight packs shown with person's rolled pack.

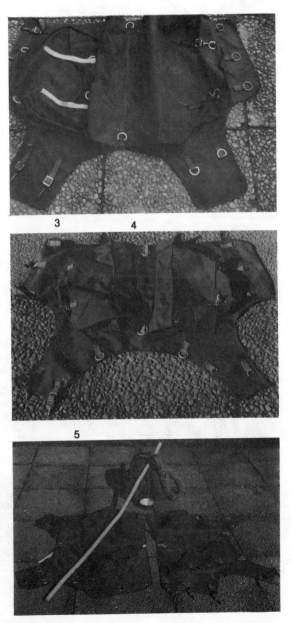

3     4

5

The pole is a training implement used to teach the dog to stay behind the leader.

Once the dog has been trained to pole and trail, he will begin to automatically assume his appropriate place behind the leader on the trail without a command.

# III First Steps

From the confines of a whelping box to the far horizons of the wilderness is a long trip. It is good to introduce a pup to the new environment as early as three months and preferably before six months. Trips should be simple explorations conducted in a safe location similar to terrain the dog will encounter as a packer. It should be free of other people and dogs, sharp drops and fast water. Equipment should be kept at home until the pup is "hooked" on getting in the vehicle, riding to the destination and spending a few hours in play there. Let the dog explore, but teach him to come on command. Young pups respond quickly to treats. If possible, pick a site with water so that he becomes familiar with fording and swimming. Early encounters build an enthusiasm that is lasting. Several introductory trips will be needed.

1

2          3

(1) A typical pack load for a dog's pack as shown must be water-proofed before it is stuffed into the pack. (2) Contents for the dog pack include: (from top left) a collapsible can-teen with patch pocket holding halazone tablets in a watertight tin, food pan and pliers; (bottom left) antivenin kit for rat-tlesnake bite; hobble made from two military straps and a piece of connecting leather. (3) The load has been divid-ed, balanced and rolled into rubberized canoe duffels. (4) Here, the loaded duffel bags have been strapped into the waterproofed, nylon pack pockets, which are equipped with drain grommets for any water that may seep in. (5) The dog is ready for the hike with a pack able to with-stand water immersion.

4      5

The pack should be fitted to the dog at home. He must learn two immediate lessons. The first is to stand while the pack is slipped on. The second is to follow immediately behind, once it is in place. This training can begin as soon as the dog is close to the size of the pack he will wear as an adult. Since all packs are adjustable the first trial runs might start at the age of eight or nine months. Any burden put into the pack should be very light. Bones and cartilage are not hardened and set until 12 to 15 months on large dogs. For this reason, it is best to wait until maturity before using full loads. That will allow plenty of time to complete and combine the training at home with the training outdoors.

Once the pup has learned to stand, getting the pack on and off is easily accomplished. When the pack is fastened the pup should be placed on a lead and moved directly behind the trainer. Treats can be used as part of the training procedure to heighten attention and add an extra measure of pleasure. It is important to notice that the position of a trail dog is not the same as the position of an obedience trained dog. It cannot be, because trails usually allow only a narrow passage for a single hiker. The hiker should be the first member of the group to directly encounter what the route offers and be in a position where the dog can watch him for cues to guide his own route and respond to signals. Concurrent obedience training does not seem to be a confusing mixture for the dog to cope with. The presence of the pack may act as a constant reminder "Come," "Down," "Stay" and "No" before he begins actual pack work. On the average, four or five wilderness outings and six or eight pack training sessions are sufficient to put the pup under control for his first trail hike.

Some dogs are reluctant about entering water. They may need an additional sequence of experience with it, using a nearby beach or stream, in order to prepare them for full exposure to the outdoor environment. An experienced older dog can serve usefully as a model and confidence builder. Lacking such help, if the owner moves into the water himself, with a little encouragement the barrier usually breaks. Once the dog has swum a few times, going in becomes natural. It is important to have the water experience be pleasurable. Anxiety and impatience about the dog's reluctance only complicate the problem. Dogs that do not easily move into water will need time and exposure. Remember, an unsuccessful try is not a failure. It must be seen as one of the necessary steps toward the goal.

Dogs vary in their interest and capacity to take on new tasks. In our case an outstanding nine-month-old pup successfully packed a hiker through a very difficult wilderness route without benefit of a trail. Other dogs have not been ready for a difficult route until they were two years old. Dogs that are slow are not necessarily dogs that will be poor trail companions. They may become excellent all-around performers, but not until they are four or five years old.

There is no sex choice for pack training. Bitches and males do appear to respond somewhat differently, but both contribute all of the essentials and carry out their work reliably. Females tend to stay closer in camps and need less supervision in the presence of other people and dogs in the nearby area. Males have an extra spark of joy and exploratory drive, but need more attention in camp when others are in the vicinity. Males tend to respond more quickly to a perceived threat on the trail, but in confrontation with an actual threat females appear to be every bit as stalwart and formidable as males.

It is true that some dogs will not take to packing. The chief reason seems to be their inability to adapt to wild areas. The confusion of random terrain, strange color patterns, extra effort and unfamiliar sight and sound never gets resolved. They may lack good depth perception and fail to perceive bad footing or the difference between a short and long drop. They may be too aggressive and charge ahead threatening another party or horseman despite repeated discipline. Such dogs do not belong in the wilderness environment. They will pose a menace to other trail users and to their owners. Outdoorsmen with aggressive dogs have been killed by bears as a direct result of an initial attack by a dog. It may be that a root cause of these reactions is timidity or lack of confidence.

Picked at random, not every human is a wholly adequate outdoor performer. Likewise, an otherwise good pet may not be a dog you could depend upon as a wilderness companion. That judgment should not be made hastily, however. Our experience with

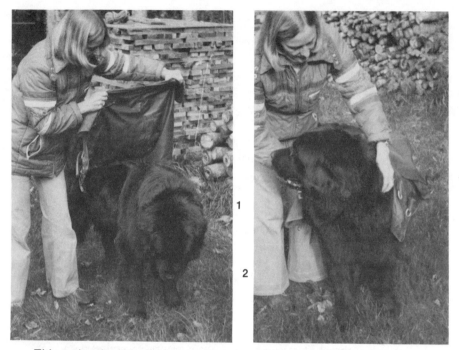

This series depicts what the authors have found to be the easiest way to put on the dog's back pack: (1) The most important part of this procedure is teaching the dog to stand still while you arrange the pack on his back. Under field conditions dogs just out of the car are excited and must be given a chance to calm down before attempting to strap on the pack. Young dogs also find standing still a tough assignment. (2) Drape the pack over the dog's back making sure that chest flaps are forward. (3) Chest straps are fastened first; it seems easier to keep the dogs' attention if you begin near their heads. (4) Attach the belly straps under the dog and the pack is in place. (5) After it is fixed in place, the pack can be loaded according to the needs of the trip. Additionally, this dog has been equipped with a coil of 3/8 inch "goldline" placed over the dog's neck. It will be fastened with a cord to one of the "D" rings on the pack.

3

4

5

the Newfoundland breed indicates that two out of every three dogs that undergo a full training program become fully adequate partners.

On the average we estimate that we spend about 60 hours in the pre-trail training sequence of carrying the pack, letting the dog find his place just behind the hiker, swimming and being introduced to longer auto trips and the wild lands environment. This could very likely be reduced with more efficient scheduling, but our approach to pups emphasizes the casual, low pressure play aspects of the activity. We want to build the enthusiasm and joy that translates later into confidence and determination. This is especially true for swimming and first visits to wild land areas.

For those aspects of training that are simple routines (standing for the pack, carrying it and holding position), we use treats and limit training periods to no more than 15 minutes. We finish on an upbeat mood so the pup's last impression of each session is pleasant and sets an enthusiastic attitude for the next one.

Of the routine drills, the one requiring most attention is positioning. With a treat in your fist, hold that hand down at your side. This will place the dog exactly where he needs to be. As the trainer moves forward and describes circles and figure eights, the pup nuzzles the hand and follows closely. When the pup is large enough to fit under the pack the following-behind procedure is reinforced by the pack's presence. Since this mutual reinforcement is rewarded with an occasional treat the dog's attention rarely falters.

The use of treats moves from a frequent reward to a rare reward. Over time, the use of treats combined with praise makes praise alone a sufficient reward, but with pups an occasional treat during training and one at the close of each session maintains reinforcement and enthusiasm.

Half of the pups we have trained were reluctant to ride in a car. This can be overcome by holding the pup in the lap or staying close, praising and petting him. Once the pup is comfortable enough to sleep, the resistance is about over. Positive experiences on subsequent rides erode the remaining fear.

We often introduce a pup to wild lands along with an experienced dog the pup already knows and relies upon. When first exposed to a vast area with no fences, no familiar sounds and few familiar smells, the young pup may explode with action and gambol about in sheer joy. He may also withdraw to the side of the trusted adult and follow him, looking about apprehensively. Both reactions will moderate as the pup spends time in the area and repeats the experience on other days.

On introductory wild land outings, we do not direct training, but we will restrain the dog and scold him if he pursues wildlife or digs into burrows or tunnels. Since we know from experience that a young dog will pursue and harass whatever attracts his attention, we select a site and a season so that our activity will not destroy a nest, turn up a hiding juvenile or invade the privacy of an outdoor experience for others. It is useful to have a long leash in the party in case a novice dog needs to be put under control.

In summary, the first steps introduce the pup to a vastly different environment, make him at ease under a pack and comfortable with swimming and ready to take his place behind the hiker. The next step is to combine these elements into one experience and introduce the dog to the actual task of trail packing.

When climate and terrain become radically different from those the hiker is normally used to exposing him to severe or harsh conditions, he must carry extra survival supplies for back-up measures if he should become stranded or incapacitated. This same consideration should also be given dogs in a packing party.

When the climate and terrain of a hike approximate the everyday conditions hikers are accustomed to, fewer special supplies are needed. Except for their packs, these Newfoundlands look as if they could be lolling in their backyard on an early summer day.

# *IV Wilderness Travel Basics*

Before placing himself and his dog in an environment that is indifferent to his welfare, a hiker should become competent as an outdoor traveler. Competence should be geared to the terrain and season of its use. In winter experienced travelers in the northern states carry blankets and shovels, chains and emergency clothing in the trunks of their cars. They know that routine drives can turn into survival problems. The normally placid and familiar environment of fields and woodlots can suddenly become the arena for a harsh survival test.

Whenever a hiker leaves the usual ground of nearby communication and aid backups he has to serve as his own support system. As he moves from familiar ground with nearby residents to unfamiliar ground with no residents the level of planning and

back-up gear should increase. Those of us who live near wilderness areas frequently get reminded by news reports of rescue missions that the urban American citizen of today regularly launches himself into environments and situations for which he is unprepared.

We are no longer close enough to the soil to build the appreciation for weather and terrain our ancestors had. We must learn to consciously consider where we will be and what equipment will keep us comfortable and safe while we are there. Everyone knows a summer hike in ideal weather can be destroyed by the wrong pair of shoes. The same awareness, when transplanted to remote environments and harsh conditions, is very important, but it must be coupled with anticipation of what the terrain demands.

The essential ingredient for successful wilderness living and travel is an attitude of informed awareness. Experience in similar terrain and confidence in his gear and his ability to use it builds that informed awareness in the backpacker. As suggested elsewhere in the text, the hiker and his dog should move into more challenging environments at their own pace. Slow is better than fast.

The second essential ingredient is proper gear. Today there are good suggestions in the literature of outdoor clubs, hiking and skiing magazines and occasionally in the newspapers. In the past ten years there have been significant gear improvements in the area of shoes, snowshoes, outer wear garments, tents, packs and sleeping bags.

Fabrics have now been made that shed water from the outside while allowing body moisture inside to escape. Fabricated insulation approaching the performance of natural goose down is now available. Unlike goose down, it performs when wet and can be wrung out. It appears to be equally durable. Snowshoes, their bindings and their uphill traction arrangements are undergoing fast development. They are lighter, smaller in area and easier to manage up and down hills. Less dramatic but important improvements in other areas allow hikers to carry less weight and still protect themselves and their supplies.

For the solo hiker who chooses remote wilderness the lesson is clear: Know where you are going. Anticipate what you are likely to encounter there. Do not go until you are ready.

The joy of the owner-dog partnership is not limited to remote places. Once a dog is trained, the experience need not be limited to a solo hiker. We describe the wilderness travel basics because we recognize the special opportunities and obligations wilderness area use offers the backpacker with dogs. It has become the use of our choice due to other interests and our local wild land advantages. For the adventuring spirit the difference between an undisturbed woodlot in Iowa and an undisturbed stand of trees in a Montana wilderness is unimportant. Both places offer discovery, stimulation, surprises and bonding. Each have off-setting advantages of use the other lacks.

We have spoken of the attitude, the gear and the experience needed to travel in safety. There is a second matter that needs to be dealt with.

Conferences on wild lands use are focusing on the impact all users have on the fragile environments of untended natural areas. Fragility is a function of soil, climate and elevation. Where growing seasons are short recovery from the damage of boot marks, fire rings, sleeping dogs and waste materials takes many years. Where the necessary heat combined with the organic matter of rich soils to achieve recovery cannot keep up with use, the damage is irreversible. The mountains, the far north and the arid regions of the West present special problems, but so do river and stream environments and any place so attractive that people collect to visit and live on top of it.

People who damage the environment spoil the very experience they seek to enjoy. Examples are everywhere. The slogan is "take nothing but pictures, leave nothing but footprints." If the next person cannot find evidence that previous parties have been at a wild site, we all gain. It is a matter of simple respect for nature and man.

One aspect of the wild lands experience is tranquility. Hikers will be offended by loose dogs charging about wherever whim dictates. Our dogs have been attacked by "pets" many times. All that prevented an all-out fight was their discipline and size. We are forced to leave the trail and hold our trained dogs when aggressive "pets" preceding their owners, out of sight and always out of control, speed up the trail to challenge whatever they find. Wild land users should not be forced to abandon their experience because dog owners insist on theirs.

Dogs should be under control at the camp site as well as on the trail. Most hikers collect at nightfall around scenic areas. In addition, we have found that most hikers are more comfortable locating themselves within sight and hailing distance of another party overnight. The majority of overnight backpacking experiences involve contact with others. The solitary camp is usually found only in non-scenic or off-trail locations.

It is natural for dogs to explore their immediate area and especially significant elements in it, such as neighboring hikers. The packer must consider his privacy as a primary right and keep his animals close at hand. Normally people are charmed by a well mannered dog who is obviously an important asset to his own party. If they show interest and seek contact, we introduce our dog. That can include a walk to their group and exploration of their people and gear. Where this happens the packer achieves the advantage of familiarity. His dog satisfies his curiosity and settles in around his own camp. Afterwards sounds made by the neighbors will most likely not be responded to.

What does the packer do with dogs' fecal matter? If others use the area, treat it the same as human waste—bury it in summer or winter. It should not be left to smell, pose health hazards and destroy the visual integrity of a wild place. Because the dogs are close and under control it is a simple matter to manage. This step is not presently necessary in all the environments where hikers can take dogs. It is always necessary where the environment is fragile and where other hikers pass or collect. No special equipment is required. Dig out a hole with the pole and cover it back with your boot.

Part of the concern for being fastidious about animal waste disposal is simply good politics. The same hiker who complains about the presence of horse feces is delighted if he finds bear, coyote or deer droppings. We are dealing partly with a state of mind. Our common experience is now primarily urban. Moving away from the land moves us away from familiarity with working animals. Five years ago the idea of moving dog feces off a well used trail and covering it would have seemed absurd. Now it is a practical response to city folk objections to domestic animal waste as well as a removal of a potential health hazard.

In less fragile eco-systems, and off trail, this measure is not necessary. Wilderness travel basics include good habits involving the safety of party members. It also involves good habits based on respect for the natural environment and the rights of others who also wish to enjoy it.

Will the dogs occasionally bark at night when neighbors stir? Yes, the less experienced dog may do this. Unfortunately, it occurs most often when neighbors are quiet rather than noisy and where dogs, unintroduced to them, harbor a latent curiosity. Hushing the dog once or twice early in the night is usually sufficient. Our own experience with this is limited. We choose solitary camps for overnighting because we seek solitude, enjoy wildlife observations and do not want to have to train our dogs to silence during sleeping hours.

Common sense tells us that dogs turned loose in wild lands will hunt out and pursue whatever interests them. This was the first consideration of national park management when they closed park trails to dogs. While that closure is extreme and in our judgment wrong, it is at least wrong in the right direction. Dogs can be taught to control this instinct and to respond to the presence of wildlife passively. Since most dogs are not trained and so many visitors bring pets to the national parks, their closure is understandable.

Harassing wildlife ultimately results in driving it from an area or killing it. The results of harassment are not immediate nor clear to the average observer. Even animal researchers and observers who are considerate of wild creatures' need for privacy have driven off and destroyed what they wish to preserve and protect.

Keep the pack dog behind and under control on the trail and close to camp after arriving at a destination. Early experiences of scolding, shaking or giving a smack to the dog pursuing wildlife or rooting about nests and burrows are generally enough to last out the whole trail experience, but in some instances it may be necessary to reinforce this learning. Teaching the animal a passive response is not difficult, as most of that training occurs in the home neighborhood before a dog is introduced to wilderness.

In discussing basic equipment the first consideration is what you wear. Every year hikers lose their lives because inadequate clothing was selected. In cool and wet environments wool is essential. In cold environments it should be worn over long underwear, which, if not wool, is double knit to trap air and allow moisture to dissipate. Wear wool over the head, on the hands and at least one thickness over the feet. Keep in mind that more lighter garments, which can be peeled off or replaced with weather changes, are better than fewer heavy garments. You need to avoid sweating heavily inside too much insulation. That moisture can also soak your garments and take away precious body heat. Wear enough to do the job but not more.

Shoes must be sturdy and comfortable. In cold climates a double thickness of leather and possibly a layer of insulation between may be needed. These can be supplemented with felt pads or double layers of wool socks. If the shoes do not fit, painful blisters will form. The rule is to use the shoes sparingly and gradually until they fit the feet. On long hikes under heavy packs feet swell and change their shape. Be prepared with tape and moleskin sheets to patch over a potential blister before it forms and breaks.

Any pack that is comfortable when loaded will do. If you carry more than 12 to 15 pounds, select one that has a rigid frame built in or hangs onto a rigid frame. The frame spreads the load better by stacking it higher and close to the body. It can also be equipped with a padded hip belt to offer more support for full pack loads. Some larger packs have emergency bivouac features. They can be emptied out and transformed into a sack that can be zipped up to cover the body. With his feet inside the bag and the lining covering his body a stranded hiker would gain an extra measure of protection from the elements.

The critical matter about personal equipment is what will provide the necessary minimum support for life in an emergency. Not long ago the outdoor experts were talking about the 10 basics, but experienced people added a few more ounces in order to carry a few more absolutely essential items. We carry 16 basics on every hike no matter how short. They are the following items and are illustrated in another chapter of the book.

1. A sighting compass with bubble level, inclinometer and magnified heading lens, with leather strap and case.
2. A large bandana.
3. A first aid kit with 4x4 gauze pads, a roll of tape, emergency bandage, band aids and safety pins.

4. An emergency blanket.
5. A heavy duty camp knife.
6. An insect stick.
7. A package of emergency food: nuts, dried fruit, powdered soup and chocolate.
8. One pair of long heavy-weight wool socks.
9. One flashlight with extra batteries
10. One pair of sunglasses.
11. One cooking and drinking cup.
12. Map and map case.
13. Pencil and note paper.
14. A watertight match case.
15. A wool baliclava cap.
16. A light jacket with hood.

If we hike where water is not easily available we add a plastic one pint water container for every member of the party, filled of course.

This outfit allows for temporary bivouac in rain or snow with moderate comfort and adequate safety. In winter we add extra wool mitts, a shelter tarp, fire starter candles, more food and a wool sweater. Please note that there is no all-purpose minimum combination of items. If we spent much time at elevations above timberline in winter we would add a small stove and fuel bottle. Where we expect water quality to be poor we carry halazone

The rolled hiker's pack contains the 16 basics for packing under normal conditions. This one, in addition, shows the training pole and line.

tablets or a small iodine bottle to help disinfect water that must be used. The basic outfit described above is adequate for our emergencies, for all but deep winter weather when the additions noted above are added.

In thick woods where porcupines are common, such as northeast and north central forests, we add a rubberized plastic canteen of vinegar. This is used to soften the quills before extracting them with pliers. Quills must be grasped as close as possible to the point of penetration. Vinegar may also be used as a deodorant in the event of confrontation with a skunk.

Normally these items for both packer and pack dog lie untouched for weeks or even months where only day hikes are taken, no fires are made and no new territory requires use of the compass, maps and pencil to work into and out of.

For some day hikers and for overnighters, especially where fast water or off trail scrambling is part of the route, we add a 60 foot coil of 5/16 inch goldline. We place it around one of the dogs' necks and attach it to the outside "D" rings on his pack.

Since overnight or longer trips require food, the hiker should switch from a day pack to a frame model pack. As previously mentioned, it is far more comfortable and the restriction on movement is more than offset by the ease of load distribution.

Last, and important for many uses in addition to being an early training tool, comes the pole. The one shown in the photo with a day pack and line is a 5½ foot young maple. Good enough for most purposes but not as stout or as useful as the 6 foot seasoned oak shown elsewhere.

Gear by itself is no guarantee of safe travel. The annual accident reports of search and rescue missions tell us how poor judgment and/or the lack of experience contributed to each crisis. It is not uncommon for bodies to be found in possession of all necessary gear for temporary survival. The gear was not used. In the past such situations were considered to be the result of panic. We know better today. Even the best disciplined and most experienced wilderness traveler can be expended under harsh conditions.

Expedition climbers prepare consciously for such moments. They train themselves to recognize and act quickly on the symptoms of altitude sickness, frostbite, heat prostration and hypothermia. Hypothermia, a subnormal temperature of the body, robs a skilled and disciplined wilderness traveler of his judgment. Instead of taking steps to help himself he will ignore his condition until he is incapable of action. Those of us who participate in far less ambitious efforts may occasionally face the same hazards, but with less awareness of their existence or consequences.

Good publications on the topic of wilderness health and travel are available from local chapters of the Sierra Club and in publications found in outdoor equipment stores. Dean Olsen, Calvin Rutstrum and Harvey Manning are all experienced and reliable guides in matters of outdoor travel. Local search and rescue groups are also good sources. They keep up-to-date information about prevention and corrective procedures. Desert travel is one problem, mountain travel another and northern wooded plains travel is a third. Local groups know conditions, what is most likely to be overlooked and how best to prepare for travel in the nearby terrain.

As secondhand information merges with firsthand experience, the apprentice builds the awareness and skill that turns him into a journeyman. The choice of items you select for your person and dog team will be fine tuned to fit your own situation.

Compass work is simple once the hiker begins to visualize the relationship between the two-dimensional picture of the earth's surface and actual terrain. He will automatically lay out the map so that the difference between "true" or map north and compass or magnetic north is accounted for. As long as he can sight distant objects or get to openings in the trees where sightings can be made, he can work his way across the country without man-made roads or trails. From time to time and at crucial decision points, triangulations can be made from obvious reference points such as stream mergers, high peaks, power lines, old burns, mine scars and long unbroken ridges. If the hiker leaves by the same route used to enter an area he can mark his way in with trail tape. This will help him locate the trail on his way out. *Take the tape down as you leave.* Needless to say these skills should be mastered before an owner risks himself and his dog in difficult and remote country. Once comfortable himself, he can turn full attention to the dog's development with the attitude of confidence and patience that ensures success.

In the past experts spoke of three hikers constituting the

necessary minimum number of party members to ensure mutual safety. Recently it has been stated that four is the minimum number. On long hikes four certainly is the minimum. One person left to perform the arduous task of maintaining life for a very ill or badly injured companion cannot perform that task well over an extended period. The third member, off to get aid, may need a full day or two just to arrive at the first communication point. However, the wisely recommended party minimums are not applicable to the team of person and dog. Most of the team's experience will be built in an environment of a one-to-one relationship. Introducing others into it slows the process and limits its ultimate potential. This is particularly true during the long training process where the unique bonding and communication unfolds.

To fully enjoy the rewards of the hiker-dog or hiker with two, or even three dogs' partnership, most owners will choose to travel alone or at most in pairs. That means they must face the hazards and discomforts with extra anticipation and prudence. Assistance will take longer to arrive. If off trail they will need to make special efforts to signal their location. Any first aid measures must be accomplished without help. Normally, the problems encountered are simple things: a muscle seizure, a stomach ailment, a minor ankle sprain or simply being wet and depressed for several days and nights. Having confidence in oneself and the dogs makes the difference between the problem experience being intolerable and being merely uncomfortable.

Backpacking with dogs through wilderness areas evokes an admiration from the hiker for his environment. The wild lands offer a natural beauty that cannot be experienced in most of the habitats where people dwell. Hikers should not endanger the delicate balance of the life system into which they have tread by leaving clutter behind once they have passed through.

Backpacking with dogs requires careful selection of hiking areas. Many wilderness areas, including national and state wildlife areas, are off limits to dogs.

In order not to spoil the backpacking experience either for his own master or other hikers, the backpacking dog must be taught to be calm and respond with control to any situation in the wild even when his masters may not be immediately at hand.

# *V Route and Trail Selections*

Recent articles and reports on dogs in the wilderness represent a growing demand to find a solution to "the dog pollution problem." People leave populated centers to seek solitude and communication with the peace and beauty of an undisturbed environment, but too often they find the tranquility of their experience shattered by out-of-control dogs. Beyond the problem of noise, indiscriminate excretion and unwelcome frolicking, untrained dogs pursue animals and destroy bird nests. They also

pose a hazard on a narrow and exposed trail. Common sense dictates that no dog should be permitted to roam on his own in an environment where he is likely to kill other creatures, ruin the special opportunity for peace or endanger human life.

A wilderness area is the last place in which to loose an untrained dog. In most portions of the country it is common practice to turn dogs out in the fields and woodlots to chase squirrels and rabbits or to practice finding birds, but people are becoming less tolerant of dogs running loose in any environment. Hikers should know that some ranchers and farmers still shoot an intruding animal and hang its body on their fence line. For the safety and peace of mind of all parties, we need to remind ourselves that dogs are domesticated animals. They, like their human owners, need to find a role inside the rules and limitations of social order. It is imperative that hikers now select places to pack into where conflict is minimized and see to it their dogs are well behaved.

Route selection first requires knowledge of what places are out of bounds. Dogs are no longer allowed on the trails of national parks. Most national and state wildlife refuge areas and most beaches are off limits to dogs. With respect to refuges and beaches, there are exceptions. These usually involve dates, hours and leash requirements. As an example, dogs are not allowed in bird refuges in spring. By summer, juveniles are considered better able to protect themselves and some field practice may be allowed for both setters and retrieving dogs.

Natural watersheds that impound drinking water have their own restrictions. These range from total closure to all persons and animals to regulations for persons, animals and their waste.

Military bases may cover vast areas of choice wilderness. Some are opened specifically during hunting season; some are permanently off limits. Most are not accessible to the backpacker and dog. However, if this regulation is up to local or regional command and allows a choice, an individual request might bring a favorable response.

Designated wilderness areas are open to hikers and dogs. the most popular areas require advance registration and a permit. A few of the most heavily used require the visitor to designate camp locations by date for each night's stay.

"No trespassing" and "no hunting" signs should be viewed as the same thing. The whole matter of private choice leaves plenty of opportunity for individual negotiation. Responsible people are often welcome to simply take a walk or even hunt. Our experience has been very positive. Once owners see a sensible and well behaved hiker and dog pack team they are pleased to offer the use of their land.

Where "no trespassing" signs are posted on remote mining claims they are observed by no one, especially the vandals they were designed to keep out. The reasons are obvious and traditional. In the first place, no one is there to observe a transgression. In the second place, such mining claims are invariably placed at a convenient point in a valley where water is available. To get anywhere else you normally need to pass through the claim. Legal or not, trespass prevails. It is unrealistic to expect anyone to retreat, look up ownership and get in contact with a company representative in order to pass through a remote holding, but it should be clearly understood that the signs may be up for good reason. Old mining claims may have vertical as well as horizontal shafts. Once the brush returns over the slag heaps, the openings are hard to see. They can also have ruins that are unsafe to enter. The sign is the owner's protection and, at the least, should serve notice on a hiker that he, and especially his dog, proceed at their own risk. That risk may be taken in an area too distant for help to be of any use. I do not advise the reader to ignore these remote "no trespassing" signs, but the fact is most people do.

What remains open for selection is a huge area covering all portions of the United States. We do not yet have a problem of having no place to hike. The restrictions so far cover a very limited area. The national forests, the state forests and the Bureau of Land Management control vast public holdings now available for use. Many relatively remote hiking areas are accessed by passable but rough roads. Maps are available from forest ranger stations, the U.S. Department of Interior's Geological Survey Office and commercial map stores. Many day and overnight hikers will prefer woods and fields where they are already welcome and familiar. The future will largely depend on our ability to demonstrate that a responsible team of hiker and dog is not a nuisance or a hazard.

Dogs in the wild must be taught not to despoil vegetation of the area or to root out and destroy its native wildlife. Droppings and any evidence of their presence should be disposed of so the wilderness will not be spoiled for those coming after.

Where do you begin work with an untrained pup? First, train in your own backyard, then move to nearby woods and open spaces that you know are available for use. Some parks can be used at the beginning of training, but they may require a leash and so lose their training value once the dog understands the early fundamentals of accommodating a pack and holding his position close behind. Most owners will have an untended natural site within easy driving distance suitable for short hikes. A pasture is a good place. It exposes the novice dog to large animals and new sights, smells and sounds in a controlled environment. Permission to use such ground is not hard to secure. It is also easy to lose if you fail to let the owner know when you arrive or forget to ask if your presence presents a problem. Continued use hinges mostly on the conduct of the dog.

The second major consideration of finding a hiking place involves the projection of a route over territory with which the hiker is unfamiliar. One of the premier pleasures of the experienced hiker-dog combination is the opportunity to see new ground in a new area with confidence. To do this there are certain steps and procedures that should be followed.

First, take on wilderness experiences one bite at a time. The hiker will not have the convenience and back-up of a professional guide service. The party may be small—a couple, a family group or a one person-one dog partnership. Strike a balance between the hazards and inconvenience of wilderness travel and the satisfaction of a wholly new environment. A "big wilderness experience" concentrating events over a few days or weeks makes for impressive conversation but poor learning. That approach tends to encourage mastery over understanding. Instead, the hiker should see each venture as a fragment that will, with other ventures, fit into a whole. This takes pressure off himself and his dog to risk danger and discomfort in order to achieve a spectacular event. Dogs learn much slower than man and have a much narrower range of responses to new situations. The best learning opportunity is a relaxed enjoyable experience. If the level of stress and tension is up, the novice dog will sense it and respond in kind. His joy can turn to drudgery and anxiety very quickly. Just putting on a heavy pack adds stress to hiking. Good judgment will find the balance between what the hiker desires and what he and his partner can achieve.

The planning procedure begins with maps. The maps must be topographical. Seven and one-half and 15 minute geological survey maps give elevation contour lines of 40 and 80 feet respectively. Just as you locate your trail direction on the compass plane, you can also calculate how much it eases up and down. You can approximate what kind of pitch you will be on for any segment of the route. In low hills this may not be important unless the load is heavy and weather likely to be severe. In the steeper mountain ranges it is crucial, especially if you are at higher altitudes with less oxygen to fuel your system. On routes off the trail it is useful to chart an expected course that includes vertical gains and losses as well as changes in compass direction. In any case, on or off the trail, the hiker must anticipate how much of a pull or a drop is in store for him and his dog. The elevation gain and loss both require more energy and time to accomplish than moving across the flat. Once the route is fully anticipated the hiker can better judge how far he can proceed in a day and how much water he will need to pack before making the next spring or creek. He will also be able to learn from topographical maps where and about how long he will be exposed above timberline to summer storms.

The next step is to learn what the weather patterns are in the area at that particular time of year. If summer electrical storms are common at mid-afternoon, the route plan will call for being below timberline or, at the least, off exposed ridges, during that period of the day. Temperature extremes will dictate clothing, an occasional heavy snowfall will dictate more fuel and food and a weather-tight tent. In some parts of the western United States water is scarce by early summer and uncertain from year to year. Local inquiry is needed to get weather and water information. Planning must include any needed food and equipment additions for the dog. Ranger stations and the weather bureau office are good sources.

No map will allow a complete picture of terrain. On the site, hikers may find long reaches of loose scree and rubble, blocking rock ledges too small to appear inside the 40 foot contour limits, trails washed out and designated springs dried up. Before setting out, get up-to-date local information on the condition of the trail

When planning your route, take into account the limitations of your dogs and the added stress particularly rugged terrain will put on them. Temperature differences should be taken into consideration also, as they, in combination with conditions of terrain, will affect the distance your dogs can go from one day to the next.

and its resources. Off trail, a hiker is on his own since no one may have passed that way in years. All maps are not up to date. Recent events may mean an area once mapped as roadless is currently a mining site, timber cut or recreation development. There is no substitute for local inquiry.

In summary, select a nearby training location or locations where you are welcome. Bring the dog along so that his conduct assures continued access to the training area. Take longer and harder trips one step at a time. Do the job of area selection and route setting thoroughly. With care, you can anticipate most problems found on longer outings in remote areas.

Accustom your dog to the backpacking experience gradually. No severe terrain at this point, or rushing water crossings. Just as people, their physical stamina and heart and lungs must be built up slowly.

Water crossings should be made at a point of entry where there are no snags or fallen logs projecting into the water for the dog to get hung up on. Currents around these objects also change and could pull the dog into them.

# VI On The Trail

On the first hike, select a route that has no outstanding hazards and very few users. It might include a water crossing, and brush and rock scrambling but should not be a test of endurance. Dogs need conditioning for arduous work just as people do. Their pads and muscles need toughening. Their hearts and lungs should be brought up to a high work level gradually. It is a serious mistake to allow a dog to lie about as a typical pet and give him two or three one-day outings as preparation for a week's hard packing at high elevation. Not only will the dog be too inexperienced to be useful but his life may be at a risk. For the first trails go to places typical of the environment the dog will spend the most time in.

A route with a narrow trail will make it easy to keep the dog behind. The first outing is very exciting for him and he will need reminding to stay in place. A hiking pole held crosswise near the dog's eye level serves as a visual command, "Back." On a roadway or open country the dog can slip past the hiker when excited. On the first hikes it is important to be very consistent about this. Like housebreaking, it is very easy if the trainer concentrates for the first few days of the dog's experience.

At rest stops some treats will offset the young dog's gloom about not being able to explore on his own and pursue whatever moves. Five or six miles is a good distance for a first hike. In mountains such a hike can keep the dog busy for three or four hours, and allow plenty of time for rests and play.

There is no need to try for anything else except keeping the dog in place on the first few hikes. The typical route will offer plenty of new material for the dog to digest. A water crossing, negotiating fallen timber, scrambling over a rock garden, darting ground squirrels, new bird calls and smells all begin to build the storehouse of experience the dog will depend upon later when he uses his own judgment. This learning is too important to be rushed. Trail training requires a conscious commitment to patience. If the trainer sets out with the notion that he will teach several needed skills on each trip, he burdens the relationship with his dominance and lowers the enthusiasm of his partner. Dogs learn significant new information on every mile of every trip. The simple fact that a pack gives him new discoveries is a continuing lesson to which he must either accommodate or get hung up. A novice is frequently hung up. A veteran moves skillfully. Swimming or even deep wading in moving water with a pack is a new sensation. Ice, sand, wet snow, crusted or powder snow, loose rock and scree (pebbles) all require different movements to keep traction and maintain a pace. The advantage of having four feet and legs does not preclude the need for learning and adaptation, especially when a fully loaded pack is aboard.

During these early hikes another very important dynamic is emerging. In his place behind the trainer, the dog slowly learns to watch and pay attention. It comes about through simple things such as the dog stepping on the heel of the hiker's boot or the tail of a snowshoe or crashing into the hiker if he makes a sudden stop.

He learns that he must watch instead of going on the nod. The hiker must also learn to listen for the dog's breathing and rustle of dry leaves or pack as the dog moves behind. Attention goes both ways. If the dog stops, the trainer stops. The reason does not matter. Often it is just to relieve himself or concentrate on an interesting smell. It is important that the dog understand that both his needs, and his curiosity, will be respected. This early tolerance sets the foundation on which the partnership between the trainer and the mature trail dog is built.

Trail training and trail work is a one-to-one relationship, or a one-to-two relationship if the hiker works with two dogs. Introduction of a second person interrupts the process of establishing full rapport and may confuse the dog about which person to respond to. Group activities with other hikers and their dogs does no permanent harm, but it does suspend the training process and preclude the full attention the trainer and dog give each other. The natural mode of silent listening and observing gives way to chatter, shifts of people up and down the line and frequent stops. A veteran dog adjusts to this as his partner does. They both respond to the immediate social environment and abandon both the partnership and close attention to the trail and its environment. Novice dogs will be very confused by random play patterns of their canine cohorts. If group activity is repeated regularly with a novice dog, the training program will arrest on the command-obey level.

Some training can be done in a group if each person with one dog will separate himself by a space from others with their dogs. The little experience the writers have had with this approach suggests that it slows the learning process at best. The presence of others always breaks the concentration. Their smell and sound dominates the environment and masks the involvement with each other and the wilderness. What is lost is exactly what is needed to build success for future use. All first step training can be conducted in groups, but trail work should be done by a trainer either working alone or working with a veteran dog to use as a model.

## THE BASIC SKILLS

As the hikes proceed past the early novice state, it is important for the trainer to keep in mind where the training is finally headed.

A veteran trail dog does the following things:
- Holds position and does not rush or pursue animals and strangers.
- Waits to drink where water is limited and his presence pollutes it.
- Hangs back and never nudges the hiker over exposed or difficult footing.
- Calls attention to unusual sounds and smells (Note: this assumes familiarity with usual sounds and smells of the outdoors).
- Negotiates fast or still water of varying depth.
- Crosses stream beds or crevasses on fallen logs.
- Stops when the hiker stops and holds still to listen as he discovers that is what the hiker is doing.
- Keeps his distance from the campfire (reckless play can either put out a fire in snow, or spread it in very dry conditions).
- Negotiates all terrain, short of actual climbing, in all seasons.
- Guards the camp at night.
- Follows hand signals and/or gestures when silence is required.

Some dogs do more tasks, but these are the basic skills needed to give the partnership freedom to travel almost anywhere in confidence and safety.

Keeping the basics in mind helps to select those specific routes and season that offer the experiences needed to complete the dog's education. There are plenty of sticking points in each dog's training sequence. Dogs will not cross a log with relatively high exposure from the ground until they are comfortable with that process at lower heights. Some dogs need lots of practice before they will enter a full flowing stream with breaking waves. The motion of being swept downstream faster than they can swim with the pack is often upsetting at first. Make sure that entry accounts for the stream flow and that there are not sweepers or root tangles near the expected line of crossing. In very fast water, the dog will lose his footing first and be swept farther than his human partner. Unlike the hiker he cannot slip out of his pack if totally overwhelmed. A hiker who is adept at river crossings must realize that the line and upstream pole work that gets him across is an advantage his dog cannot use. Under severe water conditions it is only common sense for the hiker to remove the dog pack and carry it over on top of his pack frame. In all cases of river crossings or any other section of the route, the veteran dog will follow his trusted partner. The obligation is obvious.

Most dogs stay close to their owners in wilderness settings. The unfamiliarity probably accounts for this. At times you will need to "down" the dog near camp or put him on lead if there are especially interesting neighbors nearby, but keep the dog off lead wherever possible to maximize his learning opportunities.

Another sticky point is following too closely. This is most common in deep powder snow where the snowshoe tails sink out of sight and the dog is bounding and every so often lands on the shoe. Swing the pole to tap his nose saying, "Back." With some dogs that like to keep very close, this process has to be repeated at the beginning of each winter.

There are three related basics that are best discussed together: hanging back while the hiker negotiates a bad stretch, stopping to listen when the hiker does and following silent gestures and hand signals. These are all rooted in the dog's response to body language and conscious specific movements. We did not intend to use gestures to communicate. This was one of the many lessons our dogs taught us. Once we achieved the concept it became easy to extend it.

As part of trail training we hold perfectly still and attend to whatever the dogs are trying to locate. We come to attention so as not to interfere with their reception. Over time they see this behavior and respond with an effort to listen and smell. If we come to an abrupt halt and go on to alert, so will they. They will not hold this stance indefinitely if nothing is there, but they will take it to test the wind.

Similarly, when we approached a portion of the route that involved steep slopes and narrow trails with bad footing, we turned, faced the dog and in a firm voice said, "Easy, easy." This was done to see where the dog was, get his attention and alert him to something special. Sometimes we used both hands in a down and back motion as we spoke. Turning forward to the trail we crouched slightly and moved slowly on. Puzzled, the dog hung back and watched. He followed eventually, but slowly, and at a distance

(1) On a typical crossing of a free flowing mountain river, cross at the widest point. A hiker wearing a full pack should unbuckle his waist belt in case he needs to slip out of the pack. (2) Once in the water, the pole is used to probe for holes in the river bed. At this point, the dogs are still wading. (3) In deeper water, the dogs lose their footing and are caught in the current. Though good swimmers, they spread out with the current and tend to drift downstream. (4) Because of the drift effect on the dogs, pick the widest stretch of water to avoid high velocity flow and depth. Enter and leave in areas free of snags and steep banks. Remember, the dogs are locked into their packs. Also shown here is the way in which the pole is used for balance on the upstream side. (5) Pictured here is a return crossing. It is easier to see how the river effects the dogs. The dog further left (downstream) is off his feet and swimming. The other dog is still on his feet and less effected by the current.

several paces back. Again, the dog picked up the gestures and stance along with the command. It finally became apparent to us that the words were no longer necessary.

From these experiences we learned to gesture while calling out, "Back." Veteran pack dogs rarely need the command. The other hand signal we consciously use is one we hope never to have to fully understand. If we are to return on the same route by which we entered, at the point where we start back, we raise our arms in wide circles and say, "Going home, going home." Our idea is that if we were disabled and no longer able to communicate the dog might return to the trail head alone. His presence inside a pack could alert anyone there to an emergency. That is asking much, but since our dogs have already been both partially and wholly responsible for our safe return, we know the limits of intelligence commonly ascribed to dogs far underestimates their capacity to know, communicate and act. The hiker who stays open to his dog's possibilities will learn a great deal more about this environment and his dogs.

First trips are important. They set the stage for the remainder of the dog's career as a pack team partner. Just as the initial outings for the pup are conducted, the first trail trips should emphasize the opportunity for discovery and stimulation rather than limitation and control. If the first steps are followed the novice dog already knows where he belongs, accepts the pack, is a competent swimmer and has already been in wild land environments.

What will be new to him is 1) the length of the experience and the extended time of needed concentration to finish it, 2) the actual route and its specific requirements such as wallowing through bottom land, scrambling over rocks, crossing moving water, 3) the concentration of individual drills into an integrated and expanding set of skills according to the demands of the route and weather conditions and 4) the beginning of the team relationship.

The first three elements tend to take care of themselves. Steps taken before the trail work begins guarantee it. The only hitches that arise are the obvious ones: a stream in full flow, an old bridge with open gaps to the ground below, or a narrow trail with a drop on one side. The novice will sometimes balk and need to be encouraged. Even deep snow may have the same effect the first time it is encountered. Each new obstacle is a chance to build the dog's

66

confidence or to threaten it, and the outcome depends on the hiker. Be patient. Show the dog by crossing the area yourself. If he refuses to move, recross and call him. Repeat the sequence. Do not indulge yourself with discouragement or a fit of temper. Rest a bit, feed the dog a treat, let him relax where he is. After a bit, take him by the collar. Hold it so he knows you are there and in contact. Lead, but do not drag. The idea is to encourage him and stay in contact, not to force. In almost every case he will follow. On the way out he will usually recross as if nothing had troubled him about that spot before.

If the obstacle is more than the dog is ready for, stop right there. The idea was to train a dog, not reach a destination. Respect his limits of confidence and realize those limits will expand. When we first worked with pack dogs and we came to such a test we often either forced the dog to make it or turned back in disgust, wondering if the animal with us would ever amount to anything. That delayed training and took much of the pleasure out of it. The dogs gradually taught us that when ready, they would move on their own. We believe our ignorance spoiled one dog that would otherwise have been a splendid wilderness companion.

Each obstacle offers the essence of the team relationship. When under stress, let the dog work his own way out of it. The hiker should demonstrate his respect for the dog's judgment from start to finish. It is a mistake to look on an obstacle that aborts the trip as a failure. If the relationship was sustained it provided success. Later that obstacle or a similar one will very likely be overcome. Each outing should leave the dog confident and ready for another try on another day.

The fourth new element found in trail experience, the team relationship, is served by the trail routine of obstacles met and eventually overcome. What takes place as the dog watches the hiker's movements, listens for his voice and collects experience from the outdoor environment reaches beyond routine skills. It is a two-way street; the hiker also attends the dog. Together the team creates a mutual appreciation of the opportunities and tensions the wild land environment offers.

A dog, free to use his own judgment and encouraged by the hiker's attention and response, will make contributions of information to the team. Normally, he sends a signal by stopping. The

hiker senses the dog is not in place and turns to watch him. On occasion he will break the rules by coming alongside or immediately forward. Just as house pets learn to "ask" to go out, trail dogs learn to attract attention by touching or being visible. They may hold behind and gain attention by barking. Once a dog is trained to travel quietly the hiker knows the bark is a rare event that should be responded to.

Building the team relationship is the major effort in bringing a pack dog from the novice level to the journeyman level. It begins with the first trip and includes all of the events on every trip taken thereafter.

In summary, the hiker should find the route he needs and finish the dog as he requires. Most people prefer summer outings; others will be restricted to local areas of woodlands, arid mountains or deserts. We do not encourage anyone to extend the dog's experience to cover terrain and conditions he will never need to encounter, in order to arrive at some mythical point of a finished veteran. Because of our geographic location and special interests in wildlife, our dogs are needed to give companionship and support our well being in a variety of settings. Others will need to set whatever standards are appropriate to their interests and conditions.

Though the trail dog is trained to walk more or less in single file behind his master, there are certain conditions that may warrant his falling out of such formations. Here an abundance of brush and crusted snow whose strength varies from place to place causes both dogs and hiker to find their own ways through this particular area.

On the trail, the pole has a number of uses besides signaling the dogs to stay back. Here it is used to probe the crusted snow to determine where it will hold weight and where there is no safe footing.

When hiking in heavy snow for long distances, frequent stops must be made to clean ice balls from between the pads of the dogs' feet. If ignored, these ice balls can cut and bruise and eventually even cripple him.

# *VII On The Trip*

Overnight camps and longer hikes require more effort and bring out the full potential in a pack dog. During the day it is a good idea to take several extended rest stops where the pack is either unloaded or removed. The difference is significant. With the pack still on, the dog seems more aware of the working relationship, he is more attentive and keeps closer to camp. With it off, there is a release expressed by running, a roll in the grass or a plunge into the water.

After first arrival at the campsite, the hiker needs to be particularly aware of the environment, and where the dog is. The same animal that observes wild creatures with respect under a pack may want to hunt or pursue them when he is off. As with the

early hikes, the early overnights should establish the limits that preclude destruction and harassment of wildlife, stock and people. Particular care must be taken during the spring of the year when nests and juvenile birds and mammals are vulnerable. The let-down and unwinding sensation that follows when camp is made is inevitable.

The hiker relaxes while the dog trots off to explore the site. Give the dog his freedom, but see that he stays under control. If that becomes a continuing chore, "Down" him and/or secure him on the long lead. Keep in mind that the exploration of the campsite is a ritual that should not be discouraged. Invariably the dog will cover the nearby periphery. The procedure is thorough and time consuming. This familiarity will add to the dog's understanding of his environment and help him distinguish what is normal and what is unusual. It is also interesting to note that when a mature dog settles down for the night, he apparently chooses a location far enough away from his companion so that he can hear and smell with a minimum of interference. A pup will crawl right next to the sleeping bag. Two experienced dogs in camp will separate from each other for sleep, as well as separating from the owner. These dogs may sleep next to one another in the familiar surroundings of home.

Novice dogs are naturally concerned about the new place and instinctively sharpen their focus on the unfamiliar environment. Protection of their own party appears to be a basic part of a dog's conduct in new surroundings. Novices fuss and move about more; their heads seem to come up for each sound. They are often on their feet in a listening position. The woods are not silent for humans. They must be very rich indeed for dogs.

In time they learn that most smells and sounds are inconsequential. Veterans are relatively calm through the night, raising their heads only occasionally. A belligerent roar means a large creature is close enough to upset the dog. It could be a range steer, a bobcat or a human. Whatever puts a tone of anxiety and threat in their cries should be investigated. While larger animals do not pose the threat to campers that bears, wasps and poisonous snakes do, bears and moose in rutting season are dangerous and it should be established quickly that invasion of the camp will be contested. At such times, there is no substitute for a reliable dog.

In the western states grizzly bears, while their presence is greatly valued, provide a high degree of hazard to a lone camper or small party passing through their habitat. The standard cautions concerning food selection and storage, garbage and camp locations should be carefully observed. Dogs that are not under close control have launched attacks that set off a counterattack by the bear. Wildlife professionals are not in total agreement, but many who are experienced on grizzly management and research look on the presence of dogs as hazardous. Others familiar with grizzlies perceive dogs as an asset both as an early warning device and as a harassing agent in the event of an attack. There appears to be no concensus on this topic. We have traveled alone in brown bear habitat, but only in the company of at least two veteran dogs and carrying a firearm. If a choice can be made, camping overnight should be avoided in areas of known concentration of these animals. Since the known brown bear problem is increased by the pressure of confrontation, it seems prudent for all concerned not to add to this pressure.

In any case, the back packer should know that travel among grizzlies may be more, rather than less, dangerous due to the presence of dogs. Though the danger is remote, we recommend you know about it and prepare your trip with an awareness of it. If a hiker expects to be out often on longer trips, or occasionally to be in the presence of dangerous animals, he should begin work on two dogs. They will enjoy each other's company, and the process of training, up to two dogs, will not take twice the time but will add greatly to the pleasure and ease of extended tours.

Where the hiker goes is very important. While young dogs are in training they are something of a nuisance, all enthusiasm and little judgment. Major trails and scenic routes should be avoided until the dog's citizenship is socially fixed into habit. As more people take to the woods, dog conduct is becoming a larger issue for land and recreation managers. Find a place where few others go; one that is less scenic and perhaps less challenging. Old roadways and rail beds are excellent places. Cross country travel is even better. To avoid crowds take the more populated trails in mid-week or early morning, before and after school vacation periods.

Winter is an excellent training time. The woods are open and available to anyone wishing to visit them. Ski and snowmobile routes tend to be fixed in most areas. The cross country traveler has the freedom to set his own course wherever terrain permits. One immediate advantage is the record of wildlife activity imprinted on the snow. Dogs do have the problem of footing in deep snow and they must be watched carefully in the mountains where occasional ice sheets form. Keep an eye out for glazed slopes that slip over the edge of a descent. Instead of a hiking pole the traveler should switch to a single ski pole or a long handled ice axe. Dogs have virtually no traction on ice. Once on a downhill slide, they have no way to recover. An assisting hold on the collar will serve over a short scramble.

Cross country skiing can be managed with a dog but the pace is much slower than practiced skiers prefer. Often ski tracks do not offer the compaction a dog needs to support his weight. Breaking into and out of the snow slows him up and tires him much sooner than the skier who glides along on top.

Snowshoes seem much better adapted to pack work. They offer a better trail base and pace that fit the dog. They also allow more mobility on inclines and brush and less of a target area for the front paws of a dog that is following closely. Both means of mobility are awkward on occasion. No training sequence can be completed without a few tumbles before the dog can judge the necessary distance required to keep off the equipment.

Winter for long-coated dogs is their own province. The snowshoer will be peeling off and adding layers of clothing all day to keep moisture down and heat retained. The dog flops happily for a nap in any snowbank. Short-haired dogs need cover over long tours, especially if conducted overnight. They should be allowed a blanket and shelter under a tent during the long winter night's inactive period.

It is particularly important to check the spaces between toes. Whenever there is a buildup of ice balls around the legs and lower body it can be anticipated that there will be ice forming in the paws. This must be cut out periodically. As mentioned earlier, ice buildup can lead to a crippling injury that will take the dog off his feet in less than one hour.

On occasion, faint blood marks can be seen in paw prints, even though examination of the paws themselves show nothing unusual. The cold brings the warming blood right to the surface of the paw. You have the impression the dog is sweating blood, but the loss is minute. This is, however, a warning that the dog is extending his system in order to maintain survival. Resting takes some of the pressure off and may allow the emergency system to subside. If the pattern repeats more than twice, the activity should be stopped. This blood loss may also be a function of the lack of callous padding. Sled dog owners keep their team on crushed rock to build these callouses. We have not detected any permanent damage or even signs of temporary distress associated with this phenomenon.

A dog that is worked regularly over an extended period requires a diet that meets his energy output needs. The pack dog will need no special diet. The overnight hiker will only need to translate the dog's daily ration into feed that packs comfortably against his dog's ribs inside the pack. Cans are harder to pack than dry food. Dehydrated patties or a waterproofed sack of dry dog food are best. An abrupt change of diet is not advisable at any time. If you normally feed canned food but plan to carry dry food on the trip, the dogs should gradually be introduced to the new food prior to the trip.

For the longer trip extending over several days extra rations should be included. The dog may carry an extra 10 to 20% of his weight uphill and down for several hours each day. If the route requires a long reach with significant elevation gains or losses day after day, doubling his input will not be too much. In this case it is best to feed twice a day. This is particularly important with giant and large breed dogs susceptible to a condition called "bloat," where gas builds up and changes the position of the stomach.

The dog's water needs are the same as the hiker's. They should drink freely and often. The phrase, "the best place to carry water is inside your own body," applies to both members of the partnership. In dry country, under conditions of extreme heat, you should avoid allowing a water deficit to build, as dehydration unbalances the whole physical system. Even in moderation, it affects confidence, the sense of well being and judgment. In the wilderness setting you are your own back up. People often set themselves up for discomfort and crisis by being ignorant or careless about basic food and water needs. Consciousness of the environment and the team's physical requirements should become habit. As stated elsewhere, the route selected should be determined by the balance between the opportunity to minimize exposure to hazards and the opportunity to explore new, and occasionally difficult, environments. The location of water is the first consideration.

Except for long arduous trips, dogs that pack do not need special diets emphasizing one complex of nutritional components over others. Health derives from a broad spectrum of needs met by a balanced diet. Dry food available from commercial manufacturers is probably adequate by itself. We choose to supplement this diet with small portions of table scraps. Scraps also provide a broad range. The fact that we know what they are composed of and see and handle the portions of fruit, vegetables, meat, dairy products and breadstuffs gives us added confidence that all of our animal's nutriton needs are being met.

The most important parts of the nutrition picture are what takes place during the first year of growth and in normal feeding. A few days under extreme conditions can be "toughed out" as long as sufficient calories are present to maintain body heat and keep close to energy expenditure. A dog with good general health is capable of being extended for a day or two of arduous work and minimum intake with no harmful effect. Since emergencies cannot be anticipated, a hiker needs to be able to count on good general health to provide a safety margin for his dog. Clearly, that survival margin does not offset any of the precautions wilderness living and travel demand.

Hiking in great heat poses special problems for dogs just as it does with humans. They too need to be rested, sheltered from the direct sun's heat and given extra water to fend off dehydration. If water is available let them plunge in. Allow them to rest in a mudhole under a small spring and spread out, belly down, to cool off. The hiker needs a clear conception of his route. He must know where reliable water sources can be found. Water in arid regions is sometimes undrinkable. If the distance between points is too far, or certain springs are unreliable, carry what is needed. Use the collapsible water containers in the dog's pack for him. Remember that dry dog biscuits or dehydrated meat patties will require water when eaten, or after eating. If for some reason water seems short, cut down or skip a meal. More water is needed to digest food than is necessary for maintenance of the physical system.

The accepted procedure for dealing with heat prostration is to cool the body. Without ice to pack the dog's body, the next best thing is to immerse him in cold water from a stream or lake. Such resources may be available in some regions, but in the arid and hot West, wet rags from canteen water would have to serve. Since this is obviously inadequate, the answer must be in prevention. Newfoundland dogs have been known to pack a full load for about half a day in temperatures up to 100 degrees. These experienced dogs were provided shade, moved slowly and were rested regularly. Dry heat appears to be much easier for dogs to handle than moist heat. On hot days restrict travel to early and late hours of the day, and lay up in the shade over the hottest three or four hours.

Hikers should familiarize themselves with local hazards such as ticks, burrs and foxtails. All of these cause great discomfort and the dog must be routinely checked for their presence. Ticks can

When hiking in unusually hot temperatures, it is imperative to know your route well, so that you will know the location of water holes and approximate distance between each. Dogs fall heir to the same types of problems in heat that humans do.

cause paralysis and must be removed completely and without squeezing. Fortunately, prompt recovery is seen after ticks are removed. In some parts of the country it is best to avoid grassy areas during the height of the tick season.

Snake bites and the consequences of the techniques to ameliorate their effects both have serious consequences. Dogs explore with their noses. If struck about the head or neck by a venomous snake, the dog will very likely die. Antivenom can be administered on the spot, as can suction cups to draw out the venom if the bite is conveniently placed. Veterinarians are

An example wherein the sense of team-effort comes into play. One of the authors holds onto a dog for support to pull herself out of the thigh-deep snow where she broke through the surface crust. Where a good rapport and mutual trust have been established between dog and master, the dog will learn to quickly sense special needs and have the confidence to act upon his instincts.

equipped to offer a full program of balanced aids that take into account the various effects of the intervention used to counteract the poison. However, a vet may be two days away. Again the emphasis must be on prevention. If the hiker goes first and explores the ground before him with his hiking pole, he will be the first to make contact with the snake lying near the route. Double layers of leather in a hiking boot and loose long-legged pants will probably be enough to permit safe passage. The prospect of enduring the pain, anxiety and potential damage of a snake bite is an excellent motivation to insure full attention to the line of walk. If the dog has been habituated to leaving creatures alone he will minimize the risk of a strike once the snake is discovered. When a snake is discovered it should be left alone. Even rattlesnakes belong, as we do, to a system of interdependence that we are just beginning to understand. If bitten, good procedures call for killing the snake for certain identification of the proper antitoxin.

In summary, the hiker chooses the place and the route that fits his expectations of what the dog needs to be exposed to. He plans ahead to insure that the training will be carried out in relative safety and comfort. He varies the terrain and the season to cover all situations he expects the dog to handle. Above all, he stays open to those messages his dog sends him. As the miles and trips collect, the novice youngster gives way to the journeyman adult. Dog and man move closer toward the partnership their mutual experience will build.

Moments taken for play or relaxation provide relief on an arduous trip, and may be the means for rejuvenating enthusiasm in the dogs.

Novice hikers, both dogs and humans, should take frequent rest periods. Trying to accomplish too much distance, or routes meant for veterans, the first few times out will only result in souring the backpacking experience for both.

# VIII Comments and Considerations

The miles spent in mountain rubble, threading through the flowered slopes of high valleys, sweating out long pulls and shushing through the crystal snow all serve to introduce and reinforce important information. Time spent on the trail with a dog who loves the work should be a joy. Experienced dogs occasionally fumble. Maybe the effect of this is to allow more room for their owners' mistakes. When the work is heavy, the heart should be light. A tumble in the snow, a dog hung up in a tight spot, a bounding pup putting out the fire or a scramble to evade the consequence of blundering into a wasps' nest are small adventures adding to the store of memories.

Trail training should not be approached with grim determination. It is a long process and there will be periods of dis-

appointment when the trainer wonders if the dog will ever swim or cross a foot stream without coaxing. Some dogs go through a "nodding" period. For extended periods they are there but their attention is not. They seem to be saying, "This is your game. I am here just putting one paw after the other until it is over." A little extra jollying and affection, some special treat they prefer and time will overcome this attitude. Such a lull in enthusiasm can be a response to the owner's own anxiety and discouragement during one of the flat periods in the process. If the anxiety translates into impatience, the real substance of learning and mutual communication tends to reduce to teaching the dog "tricks." There is no audience, no score sheet and no trophy for this event. Success is getting back home in good shape after living and traveling in an environment that is indifferent to experts and dangerous to novices.

The first three dogs the writers worked with took an average of approximately 600 miles of trail work to become complete all-terrain partners. Because we have gone through the training experience with several dogs, we manage it now in 300 to 400 miles. We also have the advantage of having experienced dogs to bring in from time to time during early stages to set the tone and act as a model. A dog held in respect by juveniles has great influence on their responses. We mention the mileage to suggest how important the matter of time and exposure is, not to set a goal that should be met.

Several questions always arise. How long can a dog pack? The answer varies because it depends on the general health of the dog, his condition, and the route to be taken. Our first pack dog worked nine years, carrying a full pack for six of them. The last year of his life he required trail work to bolster his spirits as his health failed. Easy day trips with an unloaded pack were arranged especially for this purpose. Giant breeds have shorter life spans than medium-sized breeds. It seems reasonable to assume that a Golden Retriever, Labrador or Malamute could carry a full pack for eight or nine years providing their health was good and they were regularly worked. The daughter of our first pack animal has packed for ten years. She, too, now requires trips designed to her reduced capacity. For six years she was able to manage a full load.

How big must a pack dog be? Any medium-sized dog that has the size to manage the pack, an adequate ground clearance and the natural agility required for rough country can fit the task. Smaller dogs are lost when it comes to deep snow, fast water and rock and timber scrambles. If these obstacles are not going to be encountered, a small dog with a pack sized to suit him could make fine company. The guard aspect of trail work is best met by the dog sounding an alarm. If that is sufficient by itself, a small dog would serve.

We are not in a position to know about each breed's possibilities. Breeders would be better able to judge the potential for the animals they are familiar with. It is advisable to avoid "sharp" dogs. Part of their character derives from suspicion and fear. The opposite end of that spectrum is trust and confidence. Look for steadiness and a willingness to please. The confident dog is superior in judgment. In trail work it is the dog's judgment that must be depended upon.

The question of where to go resolves itself after you determine what is too far away, illegal for dog use or beyond your present

How many years a dog can pack depends on the breed as well as the individual. One variant that should be borne in mind is that larger dogs have generally shorter life spans than medium-sized or smaller dogs. As a dog ages, he can still accompany the packing party, but hikes must be planned of shorter duration and with frequent rest stops.

capacity as an outdoor traveler. The pastures and woodlots available outside most urban areas offer a fine chance to observe and enjoy nature and do trail work. Wilderness is a term that tends to overlook wild places in small areas, but those areas shelter the majority of nature's flora and fauna found in the states. They may encompass very complex eco-systems with a variety of plants, animals and terrain that provide a stimulating outdoor environment. When you consider how the season and maturing cycles of growth change each area, you realize that you never take the same hike twice even if you choose the same path to take it on. Once the man and dog partnership is achieved, longer trips to other places may also be attractive.

Trail work offers outstanding possibilities for communication with a dog. Some dogs that are physically and mentally gifted, lift the experience to accomplishments that are extraordinary. When the hiker is in doubt about the trail back or the off-trail landmarks,

A heightened level of communication between hiker and dog not only serves to make a trip more pleasurable but oftentime accounts for a catastrophe being avoided. The packer tuned into his dog's sensitivities will know that as simple a thing as a prolonged gaze directly into his own eyes may be the signal that something is awry on the trail.

some dogs will step out front and temporarily lead the way. This asset is particularly useful in winter when blowing snow obscures the trail and in summer when traveling without trails. Others have given firm warnings demanding attention to what their senses perceive as dangerous situations. We have learned to pay heed when an experienced dog balks at a routine chore. Balking may be something as direct as a dog standing still and looking directly into the hiker's face ignoring urgings to follow. Trust in our veteran dogs extends to the point where we will halt a hike at any point where the dog lets us know he does not want to go on. If the dog continues to insist on the point, we turn back or find a new route. This has happened only four or five times in the 14 years we have packed with dogs. Our response is not based wholly on blind trust. Dogs are more sensitive to paw footings, sudden changes in weather and the presence of something both unusual and threatening that we cannot hear or smell.

Finally, taking a bitch out when she is in season should be avoided. Wild and feral canines are attracted by the smell and will sometimes respond to her presence by calling and approaching camp during the night. Any other male dog from other parties in the vicinity will also respond. Trail work will now take second place and some males will go off their feed. Since it is assumed by some experts on bears that human menstruation may be an inducement to bear attacks, it might be well to leave grizzly habitat if a bitch's season begins on route.

After the necessary obedience commands of the trail have been learned, the trustworthy dog will go on to refine his social knowledge of what is expected of him as a member of the packing party. Some animals never gain this refined knowledge.

One factor of backpacking with dogs that must be faced is that not all dogs will make suitable packing companions. They do not have the temperament for the rigor of activity, or they haven't that illusive quality some call "savvy" which makes them a truly valuable trail dog.

# IX The Bitter And The Sweet

After something over 5000 miles and 14 years of trail and off-trail packing with our dogs we are firmly committed to several beliefs. The first is that backpacking with dogs requires perspective and a reliable sense of humor.

For several years we worked with one animal who finally proved unuitable for the hiker-dog partnership. It took hundreds of miles and many hours before he taught us this. In that process we also learned something about the problems dogs can create in wildland areas.

At the age of about two years he broke past us on the trail and charged ahead full speed. After a brief scramble to follow we found him about 150 yards ahead sniffing the tracks left by a large member of the wild felines. Working back along the track showed

that the dog had made a sight contact we had missed and had surprised the cat, who left the area in a sudden burst of strong leaps. One cannot be certain, but the size, depth and spacing of the prints indicated that our partner had just spoiled the rare opportunity of observing a mountain lion in its own habitat.

On another occasion after reaching a high lake he charged forward and plunged in. His course was straight as a ruled line. He was headed for a scout troop across the lake. No command would turn him and we were forced to make speed over the rocky perimeter trail, only to reach the troop when he did.

Once in the early spring we reached a high lake, half iced and half free. Without warning the same dog moved out over the snow and dropped into the lake surface. He was young and not experienced with lake ice. As he went forward the hard surface turned mushy and finally could not hold him. In an instant he was swimming in the slush, water and ice. Our anxiety was not that he would drown since he was a proven swimmer, but that he would find no way to haul himself out. The ice broke under his weight as he reached across the edge of it, but he worked his way without panic into the ice sheet until he reached a solid base. There he laid both paws out in front, dug in and lifted himself out with no apparent struggle. Before we could reach him he had already decided on another swim. Bear in mind he had a pack on and had to deal with its dimension and its weight. The pockets were loaded with water and a sudden haul out on the ice did not give the drain grommets enough time to empty them. We unloaded the second dog and allowed her the same privileges. Both played in that ice water without packs for about half an hour.

We were pleased to see the ease with which the heavy Newfoundland could handle the uncertainties of melting ice and the deep cold of a half frozen lake, but we were chagrined to rediscover how easily the young dog gave up social connections once a notion to act seized him.

The last incident with that dog was the final straw. As we approached a rise in the trail he broke forward and disappeared over the top. Once more we were pursuing our out-of-control teammate. The scene this time was more serious. A pack string of two riders and four mounts was in disarray. Each rider was struggling to hold his own mount and a pack animal in tow. In the center of this confusion the dog was barking and charging at the horses. Fortunately, the distance was short and we got hold of him quickly. This was not, however, before one of the horses had slipped his load. Under the circumstances, the packers showed more grace and good humor than could be reasonably expected.

We carried that animal through training longer than we should have. In restrospect the reasons are now obvious. He had been a cripple for seven of the first twelve months of his life. His particular problem was severe and we often felt we should have him put down. At one point we moved his limbs by hand so the muscles would not atrophy. He recovered to become an able physical specimen and a conformation champion in the show ring. The long illness, its inactivity and occasional pain had taken a toll we did not want to face up to. His own survival struggle at an early age had disconnected him from his kennel mates and from us. There simply was no base strong enough on which to found a team relationship rooted in self-confidence and trust. We sensed that and even spoke of it along the way, but we had invested as much in his training as we had in the rest of his life. It was difficult to give up.

The need to pay attention to what a dog expresses has come up on other occasions. We had a fine bitch years ago when we first began packing dogs. She never performed well as a pack animal and wilderness companion, although her temperament, size and health marked her as an ideal candidate. She was deliberate about all decisions and slow in the wild land environment. Only a few years earlier our dog packing experience had been a casual experimentation. We would make up a bundle, tie it around the dog for an outing and simply enjoy the dog's company on a trip. The idea that they could contribute anything substantial, or even reliable, was still beyond us. Once that first concept of usefulness developed we hurried with a program to get the best out of it. Emphasis was then on skill building and performing. Because we would need more experience before we could appreciate the partnership advantages, our first effort centered around command-obey relations. It seemed important to have the dog achieve physical competence and to do so in the quickest possible time.

Two animals, a dog and a bitch, had already made fast progress and were well on their way toward the capacity to handle any situations wilderness travel offers. Those two were extraordinary animals. They would later wholly alter our concepts, but we had no way of knowing that and expected the third animal to take training about as well as they did.

New obstacles needed more study and time to think about than we were willing to allow. A first refusal would be followed with encouragement. A second would find us leading the bitch unwillingly over the obstacle. In the course of any longer day hike there would be two or three instances where this occurred. No amount of good cheer or jollying between obstacles would lift her spirits. She would fall behind ten or fifteen paces and plod on under her pack until the hike was over. Gradually she lost all interest in outings and had to be led into the vehicle when packing equipment was present.

The last time we took her she taught us an important lesson. We had crossed over a river on an abandoned and partially destroyed log bridge. The crossing involved some wading and scrambling and a brief stretch out on top of a large log still in place on the opposite side. It was a simple problem involving elements the bitch already had mastered, albeit reluctantly. Once on the other side we found she would neither swim nor scramble to join us. She sat and looked as we used up our range of tries at coaxing. Finally, we decided to leave her momentarily and disappear up the trail. Once out of sight we would steal back silently and see if she had gathered her courage and come ahead. When we turned back she was gone. We were two miles from the trail head. Since we had been gone only two or three minutes at most, we assumed she had to be nearby and began calling. No dog. No answer. Tracks moved south along the stream side a few feet and were lost in the brush. More calls. Getting no answer left no alternative but to return to the vehicle. It seemed likely she was retracing our route back to a familiar object. All the way back we called and got no response. She was not at the trail head. A lack of return prints in that vicinity made it clear she had not returned.

Now we retraced our steps all the way back up to the bridge. This time we were more deliberate and watched for return prints. We felt agonized about our stunt and would have given much to relive those past two hours. To our great joy we found her just where we had left her, standing on the near side of the bridge

90

crossing. She was wet. Apparently, on her own she had investigated the river bank until she found a spot she liked for a crossing. She had done exactly what would be expected of a dog with character and experience. She had moved to find us, but she had done it on her own. It is equally interesting to note that when we first approached her she was so upset that she moved away from us. We had to call several times before she calmed down enough to come forward for the reunion. She was always a good dog and a reliable companion at home. Our early training clumsiness had demonstrated its own weakness. In this case it also showed that we had underestimated the fidelity of the dog the training was meant to improve. That incident was a major challenge to our training procedures and opened the door for the teaching other dogs would subsequently provide us.

Perhaps the fidelity of dogs is based primarily on dependence, but it surely goes beyond that need in some instances. Over the years we have experienced examples of behavior that lead us to believe that communication between people and dogs has a wider range and a greater depth than it gets credit for.

Consider the matter of a dog that responds positively to all strangers who are welcomed into the home, yet bars the way for the stranger who is not welcomed. The complexities of communication in that response are staggering. During its life, humans have provided the average dog with an overwhelmingly positive experience, yet the animal comes to the combined judgment that: 1) this one individual is not to be accepted, and 2) his presence requires a stern warning implying the use of force. All that is required to initiate this response is either the absence of the owner or uncertainty on the part of the owner as he meets the stranger. All that is required to end the response are the gestures and welcoming voice of the owner.

In rare instances, always in the outdoors, some of our dogs have elevated their own critical judgment to remarkable levels. In one experience, after outwardly friendly chatter, one of two strangers opened the door of the vehicle I was in and started inside. He was not invited. The dog sitting in the back seat snarled and jumped for him. The stranger tumbled back out into the road. I had been uneasy with that particular situation, but my tone and my words had been friendly. The man on the ground rose shouting threats.

We drove off. Surely we had spoken with strangers countless times from that vehicle. We had given lifts to stranded hikers and forest service workers many other times in remote settings. While I was in doubt, I had not made up my mind about the intentions of the two who had stopped me. The dog had. I believe he was right.

Another time we had made camp on a high strip of land used for summer cattle range. This region is also choice habitat for elk, which we had been observing. At dusk a rider came into camp and we spoke. We offered him coffee and something to eat, but as he dismounted, the bitch with us came forward growling and held her position despite our admonishments. After considering the situation the rider moved on, but not before we had learned he was on contract riding a line of coyote-getters and traps. The bitch had reasons of her own, for surely the fellow was harmless to us. Once the dog had presented her view we did not urge the rider to stay.

There are other examples of responding to communication that involve only the dog's perception of his own needs. Two examples have taken place this past summer. In the first we were on a hike following a stream valley on an overgrown and partly destroyed mine road. The pitch was gentle but the Pacific slope brush was a tangle, and the broken base required scrambling. At the end of four miles and a brief rest we undertook a steep scramble to the stream lying a couple of hundred feet below. Dogs have a hard time moving up and down steep scrambles that humans negotiate by grabbing trees and roots. The advantage of four paws to drive or hold helps, but this is tough terrain, especially with a pack to manage. Once back up to the starting point we began a similar scramble to reach a higher bench above to enjoy an open view. The dog, a veteran, stayed below and made no move to join us. There was no question of what to do. We dropped back to make an inspection of legs and paws and check the pack fit. Apparently it was a state-of-mind decision. We returned down trail to our vehicle. On the way home we discussed the incident and wondered why a stalwart male had wanted to shut off further exploration so early on an average hike. We decided to keep an eye on him. The next day he appeared to have difficulty voiding urine. The day after that he had surgery to remove bladder stones. In all other aspects of behavior he was cheerful, apparently without discomfort and in fine shape. His trail behavior was a clear indication of a problem we could have missed until it was too late.

In mid-summer we undertook a scenic hike from one of the passes to a nearby lake. The day was perfect, the trail in excellent shape and our spirits high. The distance to the pass made the whole trip a considerable investment of time and fuel for a single day's outing, but the prospect of a sparkling high mountain lake in an Alpine valley made it worth the effort. We loaded up and set off. One hundred feet up the trail our giant male pup came to a halt and sat down. We coaxed him another hundred feet. Then he turned into the forest and sat looking back at the vehicle. Mystified and frustrated we unloaded and drove back home.

Three days later, while running and dodging with two age mates, he tore the cruciate ligament in a hind leg. It had apparently been injured prior to the hike and completely gave way under stress of rough play. The lesson of heeding a dog that holds a strong conviction about any phase of the packing work was reinforced once again. Had we insisted on pushing on we surely would have had a 165 pound dog down and unable to move, several miles out on a trail.

In both of these cases we were grateful we responded to real, but unseen, causes. Halting our trips saved further damage, pain to the animal and the potential of an arduous rescue effort. A third belief based on our experience is really a corollary of the second. *Pay attention and respond to whatever message the dog sends.*

Mistakes are said to cause the learning we do not forget. In packing dogs that has been true. If a little of it was bitter, most was not. The sum of the experience is sweet indeed. With our mistakes as a guide, we expect the reader will quickly move into the rhythms and patterns of his or her own training procedures with a minimum of fuss and maximum of satisfaction.

Two of our dogs were extraordinary performers and companions. They are the father and daughter to whom this publication is dedicated. We would like to share a few of the memories they leave with us. We have learned to trust and depend upon other fine dogs, but none have reached the high level of awareness and resolute dependability of these two. We hope the next 15 years of backpacking will allow us to discover other dogs that will take a place alongside Sam's Golliwog of Windy Hill and Golliwog's Katrynka Too Much. The following incident happened to just one of us as my wife had elected not to accompany us for this outing.

Golly and I arrived at a trail head that began at a high knob on which sits a fire tower. Before hiking, it was our habit to mount nearby towers in order to view the surrounding area for wildlife sighting opportunities. By doing this we sometimes had advance notice about the best place to leave a trail and locate a ridge or valley to follow. The tower, unmanned for several years, was reached by a narrow set of open treads with 2x4 rail on either side. Access to the lookout walkway was through a trap door built into the walkway floor. The height of the tower was something over 90 feet. I downed the dog and said, "Stay." He took his place and I began the climb to the top. As I reached north facing corners on the tower stairs I looked down to see Golly looking up, but still in place. Toward the end of the climb my attention was turned to the view. After a brief struggle to unlatch and swing the gate to secure it in the open position, I made the platform. Once there I began a slow observation walk about the tower. At that height a tower sings as the wind whips the supporting structure. It also moves, but if someone is on the stairway below, you sense the rhythm of their steps. As I moved into position to see who had arrived below I wondered where they had come from. I had heard and seen no other vehicle or person. Soon the sense of a rapid step was clear. With a sense of some confusion I rounded the north facing walk, swung open the wire safety gate and prepared to greet the new arrival. Just rounding the last corner was Golly, tail flying and eyes sparkling with joy at finding me after I had disappeared above the walk. He arrived in a rush as if he had just delivered us both from the hands of trouble. I moved him past the safety gate and out on the walkway. It was triple railed, plenty of protection in case of an outward fall, so I had no concern about that, but I wondered how he would feel about padding across the open spaces in the floor. At that moment he looked down. The joy drained as he slowly sank to his belly with all four legs positioned out. It was a collapse and as he made it, he moaned in terror.

I tried to comfort him but as I did the image of struggling down that narrow open tread with a 145 pound load perched very uncertainly over my shoulders became very clear. The railing was a 2x4 on each side. I could go back up for our packs but that first trip down began to appear impossible. The dog lay without movement. His distress was evident. He looked at me, then down. I propped myself next to him and began to speak in cheerful tones. Resting, and some time to adjust, might help to calm his fears.

After a few minutes I loosed my pack, stepped over Golly and took another look down the stairs. It *was* impossible. If he struggled I could lose him over the side. If the railing gave we would both take the fall. I went back and took his face in my hands, saying firmly, "Golly, I can't do it. We have to do it together. Pull yourself up and let's get started." I took his collar gently and stood up saying, "Come." He stared at me, then rose to a standing position. I worked around him and backed down the stairway. "Good boy, Golly. Come." Slowly but steadily we began to make our way down the stairs. I spoke encouraging words and held his collar. He looked at me, not out and not down. After the first few flights he became more relaxed and as we approached the bottom he began to renew his interest in our surroundings. Terra firma never looked better. I let go. Golly did a little dance of joy and I sank down on a concrete footing to enjoy the moment of good fortune.

Not for long. Before I could settle into relaxation I heard the soft punk, punk, punk of steps on the wooden treads. I started shouting, "No" before I reached my feet to face the tower. Sure enough, he was on his way to the top. My commands might just as well have been directed at the trees. Now what? He had to stop and look down in order to return. I mounted the stairs two at a time with a sense of doom. He would arrive at the top and I would not be with him. The steps faded as he reached the upper stretches. Damn! Then I heard him again. They were clearer. He was coming down! We met at about the fifth tier. He waited at a corner until I reached him, then swept on down without another pause. When I reached the last stairway he was at the base of the tower. Eyes shining and tail wagging he was there to greet me. This time his joy was unbounded. He tore around in the typical play mode doing leaps and twists. The message could not have been more clear, "I did it, I did it!"

Thereafter he followed us when we mounted fire towers. If we rested near one and did not climb it, he went up to explore by himself.

Golly taught us many things about the capacity of communication. one of the most surprising occurred on a late winter afternoon. We had idled on the trail and failed to appreciate how short winter days are. The light was fading, snow was falling and we could not determine which of the forks we had used in the morning to enter the area. We had about two miles to cover and needed to start right away. In a moment of whimsy we said, "Find the trail, Golly." As if the comment were a recognized command, he moved out in front, worked the fork with his nose and selected one of the trails. Then he halted, looked over his shoulder and began to wag his tail. Other options were no better so we committed ourselves to his selection. After a bit we recognized a landmark here and there and knew he had inadvertently done the job.

But was it inadvertent? Subsequent testing showed that when we halted at a decision point, held position for a moment, and invited Golly out in front and said, "Find the trail, Golly," he repeated the same action. Not only did he locate the route, which would be an easy problem for a dog, but he stopped, turned, gave us a wag of his tail and waited for us to pass in front so he could take his usual position. It appears he was involved in a conscious communication. That capacity usually proved to be reliable and allowed larger reaches into hiking areas on days when we retraced our own route. It was particularly useful off the trail in unfamiliar country.

That capacity was dependable, but not perfect. We recall two instances when we were led the wrong direction. In both cases, the area was rich in wildlife trails and smells. In addition we had repeated sightings of elk, in one case, and deer in another. One route formed a long maze of disjointed stretches. We tracked our way in according to animal signs. We concluded that Golly just had more information than he could sort out. One situation left us with a long search for the way out. The other was more easily managed. It should be understood that a hiker should not blindly rely on the capacity of his animal partner as a perfect tool. As aircraft designers know, there is safety in redundancy. If the hiker is down to the last system, it is because the others have already failed. At that point, a dog may be his last resource. If the dog has proved reliable it is a great comfort, but the problem of trail finding, or any other problem, should never be approached on the assumption that a dog will do what the hiker couldn't do—perform without error.

Trynka was whelped three years and six months after we got her sire as an eight week old pup. She was a frequent guide and work mate for the first two years of her packing experience. After one year of concentrated work she was wholly able. By the time she was two, it was evident she was the equal of her sire. They were very unlike in demeanor, enthusiasm and appearance. That difference alerted us to the broad range of adaptations we could expect in working with other dogs that would come along.

Trynka and I were on a high ridge in the Selkirk Mountains. It was about the middle of October when storms came suddenly. In that part of the country storms often carry high winds and drop a heavy load of snow over a short period of time. Because this is well known, the area would be free of people and we could make animal observations with no interferences.

The route was a high trail that meandered along timberline on the east side of the ridge. It varied from a few hundred feet to as little as seventy or eighty feet below the actual ridge top. Our destination was a mountain about seven miles in. I had planned to spend one or two nights there before returning.

As we scrambled up to cut the trail, a few clouds were beginning to collect on the weather side, but there were patches of sunlight. At the point where the trail was found we could no longer see the weather side, but the sky to the east was nearly clear and the first mile was finished in sunlight. Shortly thereafter a light snow fell and the temperature started down.

In the next half hour we were walking in an inch of snow, while the east sky had patches of blue, and I assumed it would be a typical fall flurry that would end in sunlight and slush. The snow would be useful for tracking if it stayed on the ground. I looked on it as an asset.

The next hour was spent under intermittent snow flurries. It appeared the system was a small one. The snow depth had increased very little and I began to wonder if it would last long enough to help us. At about four miles in, though it was early afternoon, the temperature was still dropping. There was no way to see the weather side until we crested the ridge after another mile and a half. I did have the impression the wind was up. A look at Trynka found her in good spirits and following unperturbed immediately behind.

At the end of our rest at the four mile mark the sky closed in all the way to the eastern horizon and the snow fell steadily. A little less certain about how the weather would go, we started in again. In a matter of minutes the wind was whipping the snow at a slant and the overhead had darkened. No matter. Every mountain enthusiast has been through fierce flurries. We could bivouac if necessary. In a short time we would have a reading on what was coming.

By the time we approached the gap where the trail crossed over the ridge top the snow had dropped another two inches, but the wind came only in flurries and visibility was at least one mile. Once at the gap we found a different story. The western sky was blue-black. The wind was already fierce.

Distant flashes seen dimly behind the clouds and snow promised it would soon increase. We would not make our destination. If we did not get off the mountain before conditions required a halt, we would be locked down for the rest of the trip. We did not pause for long. Our final look at the gap was enough to turn us back.

It had taken a leisurely three hours to cover the five and one-half miles and 1000 foot elevation gain. The retreat would have to be at a much quicker pace. Much of the route was exposed to lightning strikes but we could not drop into the protection of the thicker timber below.

The storm hit about a half mile back from the gap. It was a classic: lightning, thunder, snow whipping visibility down to fifty feet and trees losing their tops and limbs. At the first blinding crack of nearby thunder, Trynka apparently made a leap to join me. Join she did, and we both tumbled into the snow. She was terrified! Lightning and thunder were not new to her, but the intensity of both combined with wind and driving snow was too much. I held her close and talked to her in what I hoped would be reassuring tones. I also took that opportunity to remove some snowballs beginning to form between her pads. About the time she stopped trembling a new roar would break or a limb would kerplunk into the snow. It was a losing battle because we needed to be moving. Every minute brought us closer to the critical combination of covering snow and decreased visibility. When that moment arrived travel was over. I found myself saying, "Trynka, we have to hike."

When we started out she sat in the snow. The next burst of thunder sent her hurtling to us again. Again we paused to talk it over. We took a few steps. She was motionless. We went back. This time she was taken firmly by the collar and spoken to sternly, "We have to hike! Come!" With a guiding hand next to her she moved, but that position could surely not be held for long. By now we had another inch or two of snow to manage since the gap. Our obvious trail would become harder to make out. Trynka's collar was released. She stopped. "Come," she was commanded. Slowly she started forward. Another flash and roar. She stopped but she did not leap. "Good girl, Trynka! Good girl!!" This time she came on her own. We turned and were relieved to find her following.

Up ahead were two stretches where the drop was very steep and the trail narrow. Under normal conditions a hiker would not give it a second thought. A fall would be very unlikely, but if a fall occurred it would be serious. These were not normal conditions. If Trynka panicked at another crack of thunder and leaped on me I could lose my balance.

There was no let up in the storm. At times visibility would reduce to only twenty or thirty feet, but the trail could be made out. The major problem was an occasional stop to cut ice balls from Trynka's paws and legs. Here and there a tree broke and the ridge edge just above was bombarded with lightning strikes. My hope that the frontal action would be over by the time we reached the first problem stretch proved in vain. We could not wait. I gave Trynka the "Go easy" sign and repeated the phrase several times. To emphasize it I turned and stared at her. She stopped in her tracks and hung her head as if I had found fault with her. I moved on and looked back. She had allowed a full ten paces of distance between us and was moving at my own slow speed. Each time I stopped to check her position she stopped too, watching me with close attention. The first time thunder broke I pressed the uphill and glanced back. There she was, still watching and holding her place. "Good girl," I thought, but said nothing. An encouraging remark could bring her in a rush. A few more crashes and we had crossed the remaining 200 yards.

All that remained was a hike under blizzard conditions. The front moved on, the snow piled up and we wasted no time in moving to the relative comfort and security of the vehicle at lower elevation. The second stretch was taken easily, but I noticed as she lay back to give me room that I could hardly see her under the growing mantle of snow forming over her coat.

We made the return trip in one hour and 43 minutes. No record I am sure, but I was bursting with pride about the courage and character of my companion. As her father had done, she too mastered abject terror in order to do her job.

On another occasion Trynka presented me with the most puzzling experience and the most valuable gift that I ever expect to receive. We were working up a switchback zigzagging road that leaves the side of a lake to top a ridge lying about 700 feet above. It was November and snowing heavily in the upper reaches of the switchback. There was already a foot of snow at that elevation. The current fall added an inch or two. Despite the trouble of slogging through the drifts, I was determined to enjoy the view from the upper bench. The forest was dead quiet. Great white flakes spun down silently all around. It was beautiful. All that broke the magic was the sound of our own breath and the squeak of equipment as we pushed our way up. The effort was strenuous so we rested at each corner before proceeding on.

After a long pull we reached the last turn. I sank into the snow to catch my breath. Trynka moved slowly on up to explore the last stretch. We could see the top. The trail, or the suggestion of it, followed up across a very steep pitch that ended over a free drop of about 150 feet to a pile of broken rock.

Once rested I rose to my feet, took the pole in hand and moved forward. Trynka lay on the trail facing me. As I approached she made no move to allow me to pass. Instead she was looking directly into my face. That was not like her. I paused and spoke, but she did not move nor avert her gaze. Something troubled her so I dropped to one knee and began looking at her paws for ice balls. As I lifted each one to examine it she made it awkward by lying stiffly instead of shifting her weight. No problem with the paws, but as I finished I realized she was still staring into my face. I felt

Though the authors favor Newfoundlands as backpacking companions, there are several breeds whose heritage makes them well-suited for this activity. The Alaskan Malamute is one of these, having intelligence, endurance and inclination for rigorous activity that this sport demands.

irritated. "You're fine. What's the hold-up? Come, Trynka, move!" She did not. I retreated to the corner where it would be easier to get around her. She moved with me but lay down, still blocking my way. "Damn," I thought. "We are fifty feet from the top and she wants to quit." I listened for sounds and tried to concentrate on smells. Nothing. What could it be? Trynka was still staring. I was sure she was not hurt. "Come on, Trynka. Let's do it!" I started toward her very purposefully hoping she would slip to one side and fall behind. She was motionless as a rock. I felt angry. "Move it!" I yelled.

It was her staring that most troubled me. Like many dogs she was uncomfortable with a direct look, but she had held me in an unwavering gaze for a full two minutes. Most of the anger subsided as I considered how extraordinary her behavior was, but I can still recall the feeling of frustration as I told her, "All right, we're not going." I gave her the signal for "going home" and spoke the phrase. She rose easily and followed me down.

Back at the lake I examined her thoroughly. She was cheerful, calm and with the exception of a few snowballs that needed removing, she was in no discomfort. That evening when I arrived back home I reported that she had quit for no reason. I was disappointed in her and puzzled as to how her lack of enthusiasm could be brought to such stubborn determination, but in a few days the incident left my mind.

The next summer, in the company of a friend and his son, I retraced that route. As our party reached that same last corner and paused to rest I announced, "Here is where my bitch gave out on me last winter."

We started up the last pitch across the steep and open ground that entered a stand of trees just before it reached the ridge top. On the last portion of the open stretch I came to a halt. The trail had been washed out. What remained of the ledge were individual foot placements carefully positioned to take advantage of root holds. The fall was free. Even in summer we had to move carefully across that brief stretch in order to retain balance. Some hikers had scrambled above it to avoid the exposure. On the previous winter that breakdown was completely masked by the snow mantle hung between the low weeds that covered the nearly perpendicular slope. I spent the rest of that summer hike in long thoughts about dogs, about winter trail travel and about the follies of man.

In retrospect it was a simple matter. Trynka had explored ahead, set a first paw forward and felt it slip as she shifted her weight onto it. Three other paws gave ample traction to withdraw. Did she try it again? I will never know. I was not watching. What we do know is that the most anxious-to-please and self-effacing dog we have ever had blocked the way so I could not reach the danger point. She did so with such determination that despite my immediate expectation of "hiker's release" at reaching the goal, her will prevailed.

Trynka is now twelve. She can still follow a modest route for several miles. Her pack is empty. We go slowly and she needs assistance in scrambling into a vehicle. She enjoys swimming and manages it as well as any dog we have in still water. The glorious days of wild river crossings and explorations of untrailed wilderness are over, but every dog we have was trained by her. We realize that when she is gone a part of her will remain in the fidelity, attention and enthusiasm she contributed to every dog that shared the trail with her.

With Trynka and her father, Golly, at my side I felt I could cross the river Styx and return, but it was only with Trynka that I came so close to making the trip.

The well-planned trip is evident in the pleasure and enthusiasm the intelligent pack dog demonstrates along the trail.

The ultimate "high" of a successful trail experience, comes when careful planning every step of the way brings you to trail's end having encountered no mishap and no unanticipated problem.

# X Putting It All Together

The day will come when the hiker feels ready to head out for a longer trip in an area that is unknown to him. Unlike other back-packers who may want to arrange with local people to serve as guides and accompany them during the hike, the dog packer will take on the job himself. Under those circumstances special atten-tion should be paid to assembling good information on the terrain, weather and trail conditions prior to leaving home. A copy of the route planned, as always, should be left with a friend with instruc-tions on when to act if they do not receive the hiker's exit phone call. Local registration and last minute inquiry should also be

Trip preparation should be made with the degree of training of the dog in mind; a young novice will not have the discipline or settled attitude of an older, more experienced packing dog. He will have to be allowed to romp without pack more frequently.

made with any responsible person on or near the site on arrival. Key questions are: What will the weather be? What special conditions can be expected (floods, fire, restrictions, avalanches, trail head, vandalism, lost hikers in the area, etc.)? The hiker explains where he expects to be and when he expects to be out. There won't be panic if he fails to report out. Parties often fail to report, but if a call is received inquiring about the hiker, local authorities already know who he is and what route he was on. They can move quickly to initiate a search. Obviously, reporting out is best. It keeps the local people up on trail conditions and clears up any doubt about safely completing a tour.

Lay plans carefully. Report in, report out and tackle only what can be well managed by the partnership. The lone hiker must be especially prudent about route exposure, physical exhaustion and expected water resources. In winter, he must be able to read snow and weather in the mountains to avoid avalanche prime area.

While these procedures are "old hat" to outdoor travelers it must be remembered that most of them travel in groups of four or more to insure comfort and safety. The lone traveler is always at more risk. Camp belly, or an ankle sprain, have to be managed without help. Extra food and water supplies for a day or two of being laid up for any reason must be carried by the man and dog team. The luxury of splitting up common items such as cooking kits, shovels and axes, tents and some of the first aid supplies is not available. Trail preparation over the training period with the dog allows the hiker to select out all that is not absolutely needed long before he sets out on an extended tour. If the dog is not fully prepared, select a route that has few demands. Be sure the food supply is based on actual needs. Hiking is labor. Food intake must meet energy outgo.

Extended tours of several days are rewarding opportunities. The dog's capacity and character come out as he performs over a long period. He settles into a routine of work, pleasure and rest that reflects his ease and confidence in the environment he has learned to know.

Laid out on the ground in the photo are two dog packs: the freight pack (left) for longer trips, and the day pack for shorter trips. In the center, packed, rolled, and ready for use is the hiker's pack, complete with training pole for the dogs, and a length of cord, useful in a number of different circumstances.

Because this is a training manual, it emphasizes the full potential and outer limit of relationship between one hiker and one, or occasionally two, dogs. It would be wrong to leave an impression that dog packing can only be enjoyed by one person and to introduce a whole family or group into it would destroy the experience. Training is best conducted by one person, or one person at a time, but once the basics become habit the entry of a group or family into the activity does no harm. A veteran trail dog is not overwhelmed or untrained by an occasional week-long outing in the presence of several people. He is still a valuable asset. What changes as his concentration and communication on the move. It is largely abandoned but not totally absent. At night the guardianship role remains strong. Once the dog knows his work he will adapt to performing it in a different context.

Training the dog can become a family project as long as one person undertakes to coordinate the separated efforts into a whole. The fact that it would take longer might be offset by spreading the pleasures of the experience to more people.

The limit of the number of dogs one can pack and expect to retain significant communication with is probably three. Two veterans, if properly matched, work together so well that there appears to be no more loss of attention. The advantage of two sensitive receivers more than balances any slight loss of individual intensity. A third dog does tend to reduce attention to the hiker and, to some extent, to the environment. However, on occasion a third dog can be an asset in camp or simply add to the pleasure of a routine outing. A fourth dog turns the experience into a circus. Attention is focused on social games, such as maintaining positions in the group and gaining the attention of the hiker. It also introduces some competition as dogs jostle about trying to decide where their spot will be in the line-up of four animals that follows the hiker. Multiple dogs are also hard to handle where a hold on the dog is a prudent safeguard.

How much do dogs actually enjoy pack work? Most of our dogs will leave their food bowls and rush to the door if the equipment is handled. Older dogs, too infirm to take interest in most activities, will perk up and maintain high spirits for several days following their own modest outing.

But they do not like it better than we do ourselves. After all these years we feel a high coming on while collecting gear, packing a lunch or having a last look at maps. On the way we watch the weather and begin speculating about snow levels, stream crossings and passes. Perhaps it is winter. When we put in to unload at the trail head the snow is falling. The softness and silence muffles our own sounds as we rack down the tailgate and haul out gear. The dogs frisk for a moment in the snow, then come up to demand their packs. What will we find out there? Wing marks where an owl took a mouse the preceding night? Tracks of a bobcat as it meandered from log to bush to stream looking for some opportunities? Scat from a coyote? A deer ghosting out of the trees to disappear behind the drifting snow? There will be something. Something to remind us of mortality while binding us to eternity. The snow shushes gently underfoot. The dogs, coats flaked white, follow easily on the alert behind. We hear them breathe, hear the muffled ring of snaps and buckles, sense the rhythm of their movement and ours. We do not belong here and we know that. And yet, like the dogs, one part of us awakens to feel that we are finally home.

# Appendix

Two pack patterns, with instructions for construction are included. One, a day pack, is adequate for a two or three day outing provided the dog does not have to carry his own water. The other is a freight pack that is best for longer outings as it has larger pockets and more tie-on rings. It too can serve as a day pack but is unnecessarily bulky for most outings. The materials recommended in the instructions are adequate only for modest loads.

Both packs are built on the same principle of two pockets attached to a snug-fitting vest. Adjustable straps make handling easy. Once the straps are set all you need do is attach the snaps to the rings after placing the pack on the dog.

It is important to be aware that pockets filled with water are heavy and hard to move against swift currents. Learn to judge how much drift to expect. Enter water well above the point on the other side where the dog is expeced to land. Pack gear to protect it from water.

When starting out make sure the load is balanced. If not, it swings over to one side and hampers the dog's movement. Balance it by placing a smooth rock or two into the pocket on the lighter side. Any hard-edged objects should be packed in such a way that they will not dig into the dog's ribs.

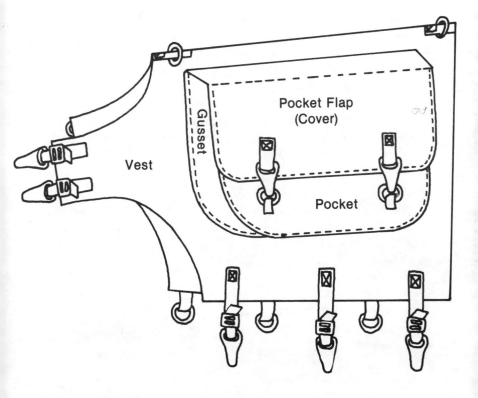

**DAY PACK**

## PACK CONSTRUCTION

Dimensions of the pack and yardage required will depend upon the size of the dog. It is recommended that a pattern be made from old sheets or paper and fitted to the dog before buying fabric and cutting into it. The following materials will be needed:

Plastic-coated nylon taffeta pack cloth

¾ inch webbing—cotton or nylon

¾ inch harness snaps (9 for day pack, 13 for freight pack)

¾ inch "D" rings (10 for day pack, 19 for freight pack)

¾ inch adjusting buckles (9 for either pack)

Cotton bias tape

Heavy duty cotton or polyester thread

4 grommets (two placed at the bottom of each pocket to drain water)

Pattern pieces include:

Vest

2 pockets

2 gussets

2 pocket covers for day pack

1 pocket cover for freight pack (single piece used for both pockets)

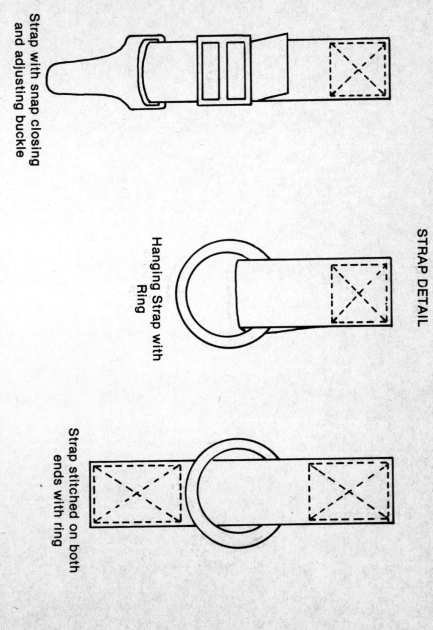

STRAP DETAIL

Strap with snap closing and adjusting buckle

Hanging Strap with Ring

Strap stitched on both ends with ring

1

2

3

(1) A break is taken for adjustment of the dog's pack. If the load is carefully balanced before it is wrapped and stuffed into the pack pockets, it should ride comfortably on the dog's back without too much shifting. A shifting or ill-fitting pack can be largely responsible for the lack of enthusiasm or response a seemingly well-suited dog may have to the packing experience. (2) Consideration must be given to the needs of the dog's physical system as to those of his human companions. Maintaining the same rigorous hiking pace in higher elevations as was followed at lower elevations cannot be done unless both dog and man are seasoned hikers whose physical tolerances have not been allowed to lapse. (3) On very hot days, and especially at higher elevations, it will be necessary to rest more frequently. A route should be planned that will also provide shelter from the sun when the hike is to take place during a warm season of the year.

# INSTRUCTIONS FOR ASSEMBLY

## GENERAL SUGGESTIONS:

1. Look over illustrations to get an idea of how the pack goes together.
2. Hems need to be turned under just once as this material does not ravel easily.
3. At all "corners" where two pieces of material are joined, reinforce with rivets or stitch as shown.
4. When attaching straps, cut a scrap of fabric to place under the strap on the wrong side of the pack and stitch into place with the strap as a reinforcement. Stitch straps in place using the pattern shown in the strap detail illustration.

(1) Detail of pocket from freight pack showing the pocket top supporters. Located under the pocket flap the supporters prevent the pocket from sagging open when pack is in use. (2) Detail of "D" rings and fasteners from freight pack not found on the day pack, allow a sleeping bag and other equipment to be fastened down.

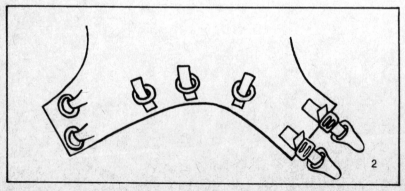

E-Pocket Top Supporters
F-Pocket Closures

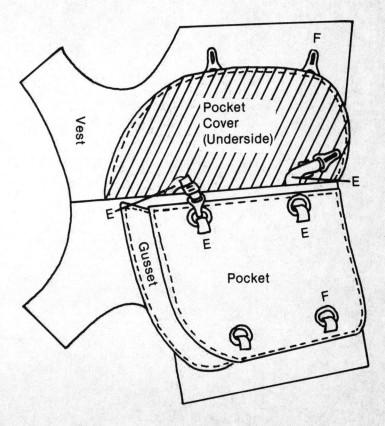

Detail of pocket and pocket cover
attachment and pocket straps and rings

FREIGHT PACK

1

2

3

118

4

(1) It is recommended that a hiking party consist of at least four members and their dogs. When one person goes out alone, even though reliable trail dogs will be a help, special precautions must be taken to avoid exhaustion, over-exertion, and exposure. (2) Pack dogs, like house dogs, will find a way to make their wants known. A dog that has been trained not to bark may resort to simply blocking the way and staring at his human companions. (3) Though trained to follow the lead hiker under most circumstances, when their human packers have lost the trail back, experienced pack dogs have been given their heads to range out ahead of the rest of the party to find the trail. (4) The dogs rarely balk at a river or stream crossing, but enter the water with verve even when temperatures are icy.

## ASSEMBLY:

1. Bind raw edges of vest with bias tape.
2. Sew gusset to pocket with right sides together making a ¼ inch seam. Trim off excess gusset material even with top of pocket. Hem gusset and pocket along top edge. On right side of pocket restitch pocket-gusset seam making a ¼ inch seam.
3. Turn raw edge of gusset under ¼ inch and pin or baste. Pin in place on vest and stitch gusset to vest making a ¼ inch seam. Repeat steps 2-3 for second pocket.
4. Hem pocket cover (2 separate covers for day pack)

   A. *For day pack:*

   Stitch pocket cover to the vest even with the top of pocket. It should be slightly wider than the pocket. Fold pocket cover 4 inches from, and parallel to, this seam and stitch a 1/8 inch seam along the fold of the right side. This will allow the pocket cover to lie flat across the pocket opening and fold down flat over the pocket. Repeat with second pocket cover.

   B. *For freight pack:*

   Fold vest in half along the line of the spine and crease. Open vest and lay out flat. Place two strips of webbing about 20 inches long across crease about 6 inches apart. (See pack illustration strap). Tack in place. Make crease down center of pocket cover and lay over vest, lining up cover crease with crease in vest and adjusting so pocket cover lies over either side of pockets equally. Pin or tack in place along center crease line. Then stitch pocket cover to vest along crease line. Make double seam by stitching one direction first, then back.
5. Stitch straps, rings and snaps in place as shown in pack illustration. Length of straps and distance stitched from edge of pack will depend upon the size of your dog. There should be some overlap of the vest under the chest and belly fastenings. If this amount is excessive it can be trimmed off and re-bound.
6. Grommets can be put in the gusset part of the pocket bottom to drain water taken in during stream crossings. We use two grommets spaced a few inches apart in each pocket.

A-Chest Fastenings
B-Lead Ring
C-Rings for tying on
   sleeping bag
D-Belly Fastenings

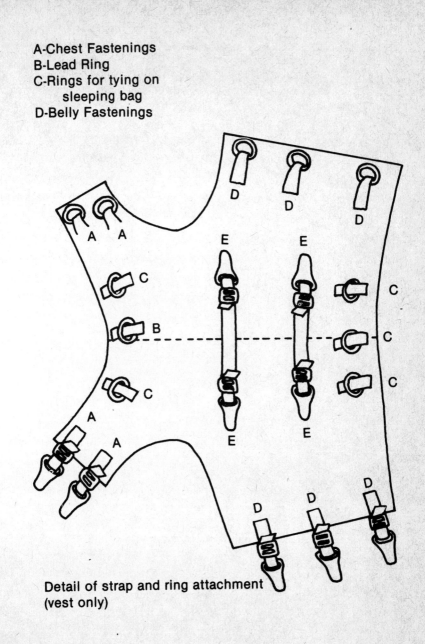

Detail of strap and ring attachment
(vest only)

**FREIGHT PACK**

1

(1) When the beginning of the backpacking trip is about to commence, and the dogs are finally let out of the camper, novice dogs must be given a moment to frisk and romp before they can contain themselves enough to stand still and let the packs be strapped in place. (2) Even though a break is taken along the way, the pack in place on the dog's back is usually a sign that trail discipline should remain in force. Without the pack, the dogs relax more. (3) A spontaneous moment of fun along the trail will constitute a good memory at trail's end. (4) The dogs enjoy a peaceful moment on the grassy floor of a valley.

2

3

4

Contents of a hiker's pack including among other things, a compass, drinking cup, hunting knife, woolen cap and rain gear. This is standard minimal equipment. Specialized packing conditions will call for more, or different kinds of items to be added to the pack.

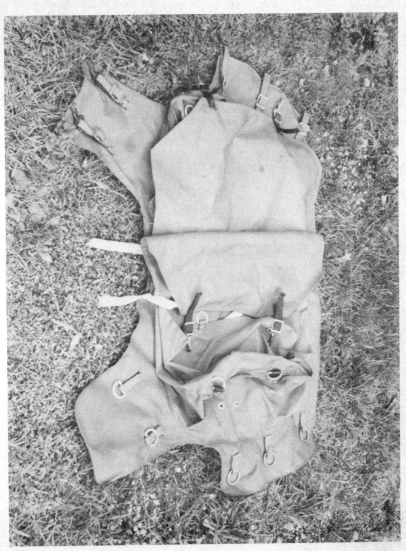

The finished dog pack showing snap fasteners, "D" rings, pocket flaps, and pocket drain grommets. Dog packs in differing sizes can now be found in most sporting goods stores, or stores that carry hiking and packing gear. When the authors first started packing, this was not the case.